Dear Ca:
I hope you :
path to Self-i
all your pufect impufections.
Love,
[signature]
xx

PERFECTLY
IMPERFECT

Cultivating Your Self-Worth
In A Demanding World

Based on psychologically proven methods

AYLIN WEBB

Disclaimer

This book is designed to provide information and motivation to our readers. It is sold with the understanding that the author and publisher are not engaged to render any type of psychological, legal, or any other kind of professional advice. The content is the sole expression and opinion of its author. Neither the publisher nor the individual author(s) shall be liable for any physical, psychological, emotional, financial, or commercial damages, including, but not limited to, special, incidental, consequential or other damages. Our views and rights are the same: You are responsible for your own choices, actions, and results.

The content of the book is solely written by the author.

DVG STAR Publishing are not liable for the content of the book.

Published by DVG STAR PUBLISHING

www.dvgstar.com

email us at info@dvgstar.com

NO PART OF THIS WORK MAY BE REPRODUCED OR STORED IN AN INFORMATIONAL RETRIEVAL SYSTEM, WITHOUT THE EXPRESS PERMISSION OF THE PUBLISHER IN WRITING.

Images that are not referenced are from Canva

ISBN: 1-912547-64-3
ISBN-13: 978-1-912547-64-7

Dedication

For my devoted father;
For always being his perfectly imperfect and authentic self.

For my beautiful mother;
For never settling for anything less than perfection in all
aspects of her life.

.

Gratitude

I would like to thank all the wonderful people who let me interview them about their perfectionism, my husband Mike for his patience, my daughter Bianca for always being my biggest supporter, and my friend Audrey for the proofreading.

Contents

Foreword

I n Japanese culture, there's an art form called "Kintsugi". When pottery breaks, instead of discarding it or hiding the cracks, the fractures are filled with gold, silver, or platinum. The essence of Kintsugi lies in embracing flaws and imperfections, believing that they tell a story and add unique beauty. It signifies that broken does not mean worthless, but rather that we can find new beauty and strength through our fractures. Much like the pottery mended with gold, I have faced cracks and breaks throughout my life, but that is also what makes "my" journey unique. None of us are immune to those cracks and hardships that we face in our lives, and I have put this book together to celebrate that we are all perfectly imperfect.

A little about me; for as long as I can remember, I have heard stories about what a genius my father was. I have to admit, I think already in Primary school, I realised that I sure did not inherit his genius. I remember moving to a new school in year two because my first school was behind the curriculum. My new class teacher asked me to go up to the blackboard (yes, such a thing existed then) and solve a math problem. I was standing in front of about thirty classmates that I did not really know, and I could not solve the problem on the board. All I remember is my teacher's very angry face, making the number zero with her thumb and index finger; she kept telling me I was going to get a big fat zero if I didn't get on with it. That sure didn't help!

I felt very ashamed facing the whole class looking at me, and I think this was the first time ever that I had experienced this feeling. That must also be the first time I felt the burning feeling on my face, and I was shaking all over. I think we can easily say this was my first-ever anxiety attack. Along with realising I certainly had not inherited my father's genius, on the contrary, I was quite an embarrassment in maths class. I never told my parents about this event. It was too painful to discuss, so I boxed it up and put it away. But it has formed some of the first limiting beliefs about myself: I am not good enough, others are judgemental, and they get angry when you don't do what they tell you.

I had to find something that I was good at, that made me worthy of being loved. I found it was easier to help mum keep the house clean and tidy, and it made her praise me, so I felt proud. It was certainly positively re-enforced. I also found it easier than solving math equations or trying to be an exceptionally bright student. My mum was very strict about the cleanliness and the tidiness of our home. Everything had to be in a certain way: the way the table was set, how the ornaments were placed, the sparkling chandeliers, the shiny surfaces with not even a drop of dust. I knew my mum's extremely high standards, and I worked hard to keep them at that level on the occasions I helped her. But I always seemed to have forgotten something.

At school, the only lesson I excelled in was music. I always got the top mark, and that really mattered to me. That was how I measured my self-worth; it was the only thing I was good at, so when one day I got the next best mark because I stumbled over a note, I was devastated, and the tears were streaming down my cheeks. Music was the only thing that I was good at, and now I wasn't even good at that! I also loved the piano, and there was one in school, but I made a few attempts, and it sounded nowhere like the real piano players, so I gave up, thinking that I was obviously not good at this either. I wish someone then had told me how much practice it really takes to learn a new skill.

Much has changed since my home used to look like a "show home". In the beginning of my marriage, my mother-in-law used to come around for Sunday lunch, and I would get really stressed out laying the perfect table, cleaning the house, presenting the food the best way and being the perfect hostess. As time passed, my mother-in-law was around often on Sundays, and I was working full time. I noticed that she wanted to feel useful, so instead of laying the perfect table, I put tablecloth, cutlery, and plates all piled up on the table, and my mother-in-law started laying the table. It was such a liberation to get out of my rigid box that I had to do everything.

I must admit, during the time I was writing this book, I often felt like I was out of my depth in the unknown and unfamiliar world of book writing, with the thoughts that no one probably was going to bother to buy or read my book and that I was just being an imposter. So, thank you for coming by and spending some time here, even for a short while. There will be much about perfectionism as we turn the pages.

For most of my life, I had believed that perfectionists were the academically successful people who also became high-level managers and directors and had the perfect families, houses and lives. Through the interviews I had with participants for the book and my course, I realised that many suffering from perfectionism were thinking that perfectionists were the people who did everything perfectly and that they did not even realise that they themselves were in fact, perfectionists.

"Perfectionism" is a coping mechanism to deal with shame, fear of judgement, failure and simply not being enough. If I can always do everything perfectly at work, at school, keep the perfect home or have the perfect body, no one will notice that I am not good enough, so I must always get it right.

Perfectionism might be wrapped around a posh, positive word to a vast amount of people, but behind the scenes, deep down, it hides much shame, frustration, anxiety, depression, avoidance, worry, lack of confidence and low self-esteem. When something is exactly as we want, spotless, flawless, and absolutely happy with it, we say, *"Perfect!"* Even in relationships, we say, *"Oh, she is the perfect girl for him"*, or *"they are perfect for each other!"* And I think the word *"perfect"* being *"spot on"*, flawless, confuses the word *"perfectionism"*, which really is mostly about being ashamed of our flaws.

So, I decided that I will do my share to raise awareness that many people might be suffering from this problem, believing that it helps them thrive, be successful, work hard, etc., but I want to clarify that perfectionism is not the same as striving for success, it is a roadblock to success, a hindrance.

The stories I've shared, from the fear of standing in front of the blackboard to the tears I shed over stumbling on a musical note, are my own versions of these breaks. But just as Kintsugi teaches us, these experiences don't diminish my value; they enhance it. These cracks in my life's pottery are filled with the golden lessons I've learned about myself and the world around me. They have shaped me, adding depth and resilience to my story.

So, as you read through this book, think of it as a journey through Kintsugi. The imperfections, the struggles with perfectionism, and the moments of self-doubt are all part of this pattern. I hope that by sharing my journey, you too will come to see your own breaks not as flaws but as opportunities to create something even more beautiful.

My intention is not to reinvent the wheel but simply try to reach out to people who are living with the inner critique that is constantly putting them down for never being good enough, feeling ashamed of it, and help them with their journey of self-discovery, make sense of what is going on, so they can let go of constantly focusing on what they believe to be their shortcomings, see their achievements and qualities that make them a worthy human being, be empowered to live the life they deserve.

I hope you find parts that relate to you in this book and enjoy the read and exercises, which will take you through self-discovery and reflection and start doing your future self a favour by implementing the positive changes.

"I would like to take you on a journey from where you are now to where you want to be, help you overcome the barriers and the fears that are holding you back from achieving your full potential. Let's work together through this book to get you there".

The aim of this book

Many people perceive perfectionism as a strength to be proud of, and their high standards are the reason behind their success in different areas of their lives. However, setting up those relentlessly high standards and demands upon yourself or others can significantly impact your well-being and those around you.

Perfectionism can lead to frustration, worry, social isolation, depression and a persistent sense of failure both in your professional and private life.

- Understanding the negative effects of Perfectionism and the reasons behind the stress, anxiety and low mood it causes.
- Understand anxiety and fear, similarities and the differences.

- Cognitive Behavioural Therapy (CBT) principles and the types of Perfectionism; specific thoughts/beliefs, emotions and behaviour of a Perfectionist, and insight into the linked psychological issues.
- Identifying the Maintenance Cycle, why does it keep happening.
- Techniques to change perspectives and reduce negative emotions and alter unhelpful behaviour.
- Revisiting your personal values and what really matters.
- Confidence and self-esteem building.
- Assertive communication.
- Self-compassion vs. Self-criticism.
- Practical strategies, including Mindfulness techniques, to create your happier self and improve your relationships.
- Gratitude and journaling.
- The essentials of Happiness.
- Tools and resources you can use to implement your new knowledge straight away to cope with stress and anxiety caused by traits of perfectionism.

In this book, we'll explore the noble - yet mostly impossible-to-achieve – goal of perfectionism. We'll debunk myths and misconceptions, provide tangible solutions that can be applied to everyday life, and create a space of reflection, compassion, and understanding. Together, we'll clear up the cognitive clutter to level up our work, creativity and confidence - all from the comfort of your own couch!

Here, you will find everything that will help you understand Perfectionism and a step-by-step guide with forms to fill in to help you break free from the chains of perfectionism and finally be liberated to pursue your life's purposes to find happiness and fulfilment.

If you're tired of chasing the impossible demands you put upon yourself and others, come learn how to bid perfectionism adieu once and for all. I will be with you all the way through!

Email: info@mindandmood.co.uk
Phone: 01277 424 911
www.mindandmood.co.uk

Aylin's Practical Daily Journal "TRANSFORMATION THROUGH THE POWER OF QUOTES: *Daily Mindset Quotes, 5 Minute Planning and Gratitude Journals to Transform Challenges into Triumphs*" is based on psychologically proven methods as well, and available on Amazon: https://amzn.to/3SD8sED

You can download free e-books, worksheets, audio-guided meditation and attention training at https://www.mindandmood.co.uk/resources/

Are You A Perfectionist?

Do you find yourself constantly trying to reach your own very high standards/demands?	Yes	No
Do you often pay a high price while trying to reach your high standards/demands? (Little sleep, lack of focus, tiredness, no time for yourself, family or friends)	Yes	No
In which areas do you find your standards are really high:		
Professional and/or academic work	Yes	No
Personal appearance	Yes	No
Sports, physical activity	Yes	No
Intimate relationships and friendships	Yes	No
Housework/cleaning	Yes	No
Parenting	Yes	No
Entertainment	Yes	No
Social life	Yes	No
Health	Yes	No
Writing and speaking	Yes	No
Hygiene and health	Yes	No
Do you get anxious, frustrated or overwhelmed while trying to reach your standards?	Yes	No
Do you often become snappy or angry	Yes	No
Do your standards slow you down and you end up spending too much time on tasks at hand?	Yes	No
Do you feel useless and/or like a failure when you don't reach these standards?	Yes	No
Do your success and accomplishments mean everything to you?	Yes	No
Does your sense of worth and self-esteem depend on your successes?	Yes	No
Do you dismiss your achievements once you reach your goals and think anyone can do them? No big deal.	Yes	No
Are you excessively organised?	Yes	No
Do you always seek other people's opinions before making decisions?	Yes	No
Do you always focus on your mistakes, dwell on them and beat yourself up?	Yes	No
Do you often find yourself procrastinating?	Yes	No
Do you find it hard to delegate work because you don't trust others?	Yes	No
Are you afraid of making mistakes?	Yes	No
Do you find criticism highly offensive?	Yes	No
Do you feel that other people measure your performance and have higher expectations from you?	Yes	No
Do you put pressure on yourself to achieve what you perceive that others are expecting of you?	Yes	No
Do you expect others to hold high standards as yours?	Yes	No

If you have answered "yes" to more than 15 questions and it is causing you anxiety, then this book can help.

Chapter 1

Chasing Perfection: How High?

What is wrong with having goals and **wanting to succeed?** *Nothing, right?*

Have you ever thought about how we get conditioned to good behaviour and success from a very young age? We get neat and shiny stars in the nursery for our good behaviour, and we get praise or perhaps even presents when we get good marks and approval from our parents. We get promotions, bonuses, and pay raises when we do good work, pat on the back and acknowledgement.

Success is highly rewarded in our society; we get the power to buy things we desire and show off our success with the cars we drive, houses we live in, and the schools our children attend. *And that is all fine as long as our mental health is not at stake!*

In our modern society, we learn to build our happiness from outside in and make it dependent on the image of success. You might at some point have thought about someone: *"She has everything, and everything in her life is just so perfect!"*. Many people look up to successful and wealthy people, sometimes even with jealousy. Perhaps that is what makes the word *"perfectionism"* somewhat sound positive, but in fact, it is a word that has many negative beliefs, emotions and habits hidden behind it. Perfectionism is a fancy word for fear: fear of failure, fear of being judged, fear of not being enough, shame, guilt, anxiety and depression.

When is it that we start paying a high price for being a successful professional, a good son or daughter, a good partner, a good parent, a good friend, a good colleague, a good member of society, a good sports person, thin, good looking, healthy, neat, tidy, thoughtful, great company and the list goes on. Is it realistic, humanly possible to be all these things or to be flawless even in one of these, let alone all?

When I look around and pay attention, I see perfectionism everywhere: in my husband, myself, my friends, my colleagues, my daughter, my family, my clients, the list is endless. They often hold standards and demands in one or several areas on themselves and/or others that are simply impossible to keep up humanly.

My mother would always find pride in her immaculate house. Never a drop of dust, all ornaments always in perfect order, dinner plates set with flowers on the left side, cutlery placed on the perfectly folded napkins, and glasses in the right order. My mother used to spend two days preparing for the dinner guests.

At those times, many things were not readily available from the supermarkets. Even the mayonnaise could not be bought ready-made, and I used to help mum make it while slowly dropping the olive oil into the mix she was whisking with a fork. The mezes would look absolutely scrumptious, and the table would look impressive. This was always important for my mother. We were not allowed to touch the food or the dessert before they were put on the table in their glorious full beauty. Once the guests broke the magic of the perfectness of the dish, then we children could have some too.

In Perspective

Striving for achievements	Perfectionism
<ul><li>Self-worth built from inside resources.</li><li>Drive for accomplishment.</li><li>If not succeeded, learn and apply the learning in the future.</li><li>Focus on wins and positive outcomes.</li><li>Flexible growth mindset.</li><li>Joy in line with personal values.</li></ul>	<ul><li>Self-worth is dependent on achievements and success.</li><li>Highly critical self.</li><li>Fear of failure.</li><li>Focus on flaws.</li><li>Rigid mindset.</li><li>All-or-nothing outlook.</li><li>Relentlessly high standards.</li><li>Avoid mistakes.</li><li>Fear of being judged by others.</li></ul>

I remember my mother staying up till late at night after everyone went to sleep to keep her home clean, nice and orderly. From a very early age, I realised that if the house was clean and tidy, it was a very good thing. It also made my mother happy, and I got a lot of praise from her for helping, which also made me feel good about myself.

I have this image of my mother stressed and exhausted with the vacuum cleaner, and I always wanted to lessen her stress and make her feel better by helping. Just a little note that we actually had a cleaning lady weekly, but my mother would also clean before and after the cleaning lady. And the following days of the week!

My siblings and I are all grown-up adults now, but when we go to visit my mother, we all know that when you set the table, you have to use the correct plates with flowers towards the same direction, along with many other things that my mother would not tolerate if done differently.

My childhood was also full of stories about how intelligent my father was from a very young age. As I was growing up, he had a high-level management role at IBM, which in the 1970s was a big deal. I don't recall seeing my father ever anxious though. He was always quite a laid-back person, according to my mum, sometimes too laid back. For me, my dad was as close to perfect as anyone could get.

Looking at my childhood, I was oblivious to the world outside until I was 6. I guess you can call that *"living in the la la land"*. I just loved singing and dancing and performed for each family member and all our guests at every chance I got. This was reinforced by the fact that they clapped and cheered.

I would grab any microphone, even if it was a wedding party, and start singing. I loved it and thought I had a good voice because people seemed to like listening to me. Looking back, I started identifying singing as something that made me special and acceptable, especially in senior girls' school, where I was boarding. However, if I got anything less than the top mark in music, I used to get really upset and tearful.

I didn't really care about the marks in maths or literature, history, etc., because I knew I would never reach the bar of a genius like my father, so what to do but give up on that, right? But music was and always had to be top mark. I can see now what kind of fear I was hiding behind, not being good at music. Being able to sing (and I can assure you it was more about my confidence to stand up and sing than my voice) helped build my self-esteem in a school of about 2000 students. And if I didn't get the top mark, I felt everyone would think I was flawed and I wouldn't be worthy of being friends with.

For sure, I had some wonderful friends, who still are my friends today, but there were, without a doubt, also many girls who did not like me, however that means they must have noticed me in order not to like me. And a government girls' boarding school can be quite gruesome, and perhaps music saved me in a way.

Many of my clients say their parents never pressured them to succeed or be the best in school, and so on, and they don't understand why they put such impossible standards upon themselves. The thing is, including myself, we believe that perfectionism is all about success in school and business life. The belief of *"They are perfectionists, but it pays off. They get the best marks, high-paying successful jobs!"*

No! Perfectionism can creep in around many aspects of a perfectionist's life. It can come as having the tidiest/cleanest house, being the perfect entertainer, making the perfect presentations, having the perfect body.

It is not about the best marks, the best job, the best body, the best clothes… It is about how much of your self-worth you put into these concepts. Your self-worth, your self-esteem wrapped inside a posh word. *"Perfectionism comes with a lot of emotional pain, shame, anxiety, fear of failing, not being enough, frustration, anger, disappointment, self-criticism and depression"* in the name of trying to feel "enough and worthy". Worthy of love, worthy of care, worthy of success.

I saw a job advertisement the other day, and I was mortified to see that on the job description, they wrote, *"We don't mind you if you are a perfectionist"*. These are the type of narratives that wraps perfectionism into something positive that it absolutely is not!

Burnout across gender, age and socioeconomic background has increased over the past few years and worsened after COVID-19, according to Dr. Gordon Parker, professor of psychiatry at the University of New South Wales in Australia. Dr Parker suggests that perfectionists are particularly at risk of stress, anxiety, exhaustion and burnout.

The thing about perfectionism is that when you occasionally reach the high bar and achieve what you have been working for, you do not take time to celebrate and enjoy that achievement and the hard work it took to get there. In fact, you dismiss it as *"no big deal, anyone can do it"*, and you raise the bar even higher, so the race starts again. And it must be said that to reach these relentlessly high standards, you give up much time from the things you enjoy: self-care, sleep, socialising and quality time with loved ones. So, the price you pay keeps increasing in correlation with the bar.

If you find yourself under constant stress and anxious to reach the all-but-nothing, must reach high standards you put upon yourself or believe that others expect of you, then you might just be at a point where you are no longer striving for success, but *"Perfectionism"* is making your life and of those around you, miserable.

One of my clients told me that she did not think her team were doing their best, so she ended up doing most of the work herself, working many hours, frustrated and stressed until she felt the project was absolutely perfect. She didn't have time to spend with her partner, meet up with her friends, or even exercise. She then ended up beating herself up if the client was not completely satisfied. Does this sound familiar?

Main Characteristics	Type of Negative Thoughts
• Self-worth depends on achievements. • Focusing on mistakes rather than wins. • Unrealistically high standards (causing to pay a high price). • Highly critical inner voice when making mistakes or not reaching those standards. • Cannot tolerate uncertainty and need to know results or not knowing when it is good enough, doing other colleagues' work on the project too. • Dismissing achievements. • Continues sense of failure and sacrifice.	• I must always deliver perfect results. • I am such an idiot for not knowing the answer in the meeting. • They will think I don't deserve this position; I don't trust others to do as good a job as I do, so I end up doing it all. I must never say no, or they'll think I am incapable. • I must have the most entertaining conversations; otherwise, people will think I'm strange, not good enough, stupid. • If I don't dress perfectly right for the occasion, people will laugh at me. • If I am overweight, no one will like me. • I must always have the perfect body/perfect clothes.

The fundamental issue with perfectionism is that our self-worth depends on our successes in reaching high standards, so you can see how fragile our self-esteem becomes. However, when we succeed in getting a job or promotion, it is very short-lived and even dismissed - anyone could do it, no big deal. The bar of demand keeps getting higher. We dwell on the smallest mistakes rather than wins, and the highly critical inner voice becomes louder. This constant sense of failure, of course, has a detrimental impact on our self-esteem and confidence.

As I mentioned previously, when I started this book, I just wanted it to be a light and helpful reading and some regular practice to move you from where you do not wish to be towards where you want to be in your life.

I am not going to go for the Oxford dictionary or textbook description of what perfectionism is with references from research papers; instead, I decided to write down the sentences that my perfectionist clients, friends and people I have interviewed who have described perfectionism as they experienced it, and you can make your own mind up.

Perfectionism is:

- Setting such relentless standards upon yourself and others that it continuously steals the joy from your life and leaves you with constant sadness, frustration, anger, exhaustion and guilt.

- Always trying to attain to a level of the highest merit of 100%; anything else is unacceptable.

- Trait to strive for an achievable, self-imposed outcome, which is harmful because the realm of perfect does not exist.

- Constantly working towards higher and better, not giving up until it is all completed to the perfect level to maintain your image, so you burn yourself up.

- Constantly striving for something to be as perfect as possible, often to the detriment of not completing a project and or accepting that it is good enough.

- It's a painful obsession with getting anything and everything right the first time when, sometimes, good enough is good enough. To me, it means always going the extra mile to get things as near perfect as possible, which is a waste of energy.

Do any of the above resonate with you? What would your description of *"Perfectionism"* be?

- I think perfectionism is

_____
_____
_____
_____

Pursuing unrealistic standards can significantly impact your well-being and others around you, leading to frustration, stress, worry, and a constant sense of "fear of failure," failing yourself, and failing others.

The problem with pursuing perfection is that you will never be happy with your achievements. You will always be looking to improve, and this can lead to anxiety, depression, and even physical health problems.

You can break the cycle, write a new future for yourself, and change the ripple effect on others!

Is my perfectionism about me or others? *It can even be perceived!*

Hewitt and Flett's (Hewitt et al., 1996) model suggests three dimensions of Perfectionism. Although there may be three main types, you may find yourself being affected by two or across all of them. They share a common goal: the pursuit of flawlessness. Many of my clients report that they often experience all three depending on the situations they are in.

Self-oriented perfectionism is about constantly trying to reach your own relentlessly high demands with no leeway, and it is internally motivated. When you occasionally reach those unrealistically high standards, the bar rises even higher. I must get into Cambridge, I must send my children to private school, I should be having my own house by now.

My client Ellie had set her heart to go to the University of Cambridge. This was the only option she could possibly accept, and she was suffering from anxiety that if she did not get into this university, it meant that she failed herself, her parents and her teachers, who believed in her. The anticipatory fear of failure and fear of shame were causing her huge anxiety. Her second choice was not even an option; it was *Cambridge or Failure*.

Other-oriented perfectionism is the thought that others do not have high standards as we do and cannot do the task at hand as well as we can. Several of my clients at the high level of management report that they often stay until late in order to complete a report, a project, a budget or a presentation doing everyone else's parts, or what might have been missed until it is perfect. They also complain that others just don't care, and they have low standards. This type of perfectionism is also internally motivated.

Socially prescribed perfectionism is about what you might think other people's expectations are of you and is externally motivated. Ellie, whom I mentioned earlier, was both self-oriented as well as a socially prescribed perfectionist. She was extremely worried about disappointing her parents and her teachers if she did not get into her first choice of university, and she could not bear the thought of facing them if she did not succeed.

Perfectionists often view high standards and self-criticism as positive traits. They tend to believe that it is the drive behind their motivation and that it would keep them going. Often, people are proud to have high standards. But if holding these high standards and demands are causing anxiety, leading to missing the small joys of the present moment because we are so worried about not getting it perfect in the future, then it is a roadblock, not a motivating force or striving for improvement and self-growth.

What you think others are expecting of you is also a type of mind reading. You might think if you say no to a workload, people will think you are not good enough or not capable of handling your work. Mind reading has a large correlation with serious mental health problems.

Curran & Hill (2019) analysed data gathered over the years of 40000 college students and found that perfectionism doubled from 1989 to 2017 from 9% to 18%, and by 2050, they predict 1 in 3 young people is expected to be having mental health problems due to unrelenting need to meet what they perceive to be other people's expectations academically, professionally and in their private lives (Psychological Bulletin, 2019).

Another 2017 study revealed that socially perceived type of perfectionism was also positively related to a range of psychological problems such as social phobia, body

11

dissatisfaction, bulimia nervosa and had the largest relationship of other types of perfectionism with depression and anxiety (Limburg et al., 2017)

We are not born perfect (Even though some of our parents may think so 😊)! And we are certainly not born as perfectionists. Perfectionism is something we learn through our environment, socially constructed and perhaps there is some genetics involved. There can very well be many reasons, including positive reinforcement, praise, promotion, pay rise etc. Especially in today's society.

It affects the way we view ourselves, others and the world. Perfectionism isn't about high standards. It's about *"unrealistically high"* standards and demands. If you strive for excellence, you are more likely to appreciate and be happy with your achievements, accept criticism or your mistakes bravely, and use them as a part of your growth.

Think about the effects of social media on many people, especially young people. The world of illusions! We know that when we are rewarded, the brain releases *"Dopamine,"* the feel-good hormone. Every time someone gets a "like" on their post on social media, the brain releases this hormone, so you can see how people can become addicted to the "likes" on digital media.

I heard a story the other day that someone who had taken part in a running competition fell into a pit of water and was disqualified. Yet, the person posted the event on social media with a thumbs up, a happy picture, saying, *"I totally smashed it today!"*.

Some of my perfectionist clients stated they reach their high standards quite often; however tough and unrealistic people may think. The question is, *"What is the price?"*. Are you paying a high price while trying to reach those high standards?

Perhaps you are spending long nights preparing a project or a report, losing sleep, time with family, time with your friends or for yourself? How about the anxiety you are experiencing?

You may get praise for this project, but how exhausted are you while constantly trying to reach your high, relentless standards and raising the bar a little bit higher each time? Often, you are not alone in paying the high price either. Other people around you, colleagues and family, are most likely to be affected by your perfectionist ways.

Perfectionists have a view of the world that encourages the pursuit of relentlessly high standards and a positive association between these standards and a conditional sense of self-acceptance and self-worth.

While many cultures suggest that perfectionism is a positive concept, a lot of recent studies show that setting unrealistic expectations has unhealthy results in our physical, emotional, social and mental wellbeing. People often think perfectionism is a positive thing, but it can also get in the way of living a well-balanced and meaningful life.

Perfectionist thinking, as positive as it sounds in many cultures, hides many negative thoughts, emotions and behaviour and can be extremely debilitating. We are taught the most important qualities to have are excellence and high standards. However, I define perfectionism as ***"the pursuit of flawlessness, with the potential destructive consequences that come along with it."***

You may be experiencing perfectionism in one or several different areas of your life. Some of my clients reported that they experience all at the same time, some are more concerned about just one area, and most of the time, it turns out to be in their professional lives, but some also report that they feel it is affecting all areas of their lives. They find themselves in a constant state of stress and anxiety.

I think I will have to draw attention to our modern society at this point. We all start learning about this from an early age at school. When we do well and get good grades, we get awarded, we get respect from teachers and our peers, and we hear how proud our parents are of our work. This also continues into our adult lives when we get a job, get promoted when we do well, and have a pay rise. It gives us a sense of pride to be successful.

Why is being successful so important? Often, it is because we can buy a nice house and car, send our children to good schools, go on nice holidays, afford private healthcare and many other luxurious things that the world can offer. So how come all the rich people are not all fulfilled and happy?

Research at Harvard University showed that when they asked people earning $30K pa., they said they would be happy if they earned $50, and people earning $100K said they would be happy if they were earning $250K pa. So, are our minds tricking us where and how we find happiness?

It also turned out that $75K was the threshold to cover all the basic needs and some more. So, imagine that you are earning enough to have a nice house, a car, go on family holidays perhaps once a year, you are not worried about food on the table and can afford nice clothes, any earning above that does not seem to make a huge difference in the level of happiness. We will look further into this concept in our *"values"* chapter.

How do I know what areas are involved in my perfectionist thinking? *It can be one, can be two or more.*

In our society, there is a great emphasis on perfectionism. We are taught from a young age that in order to be successful, we must be perfect. This pursuit of perfection can lead to anxiety and depression when we inevitably fall short.

The lovely people who were kind enough to let me interview them indicated that they found themselves setting high standards in more than just one of the following areas. Let's explore!

Professional and/or academic work: You are more likely to be beating yourself up for grades other than the highest or constant professional success. You may recently have got a promotion, but if you do not get promoted next time, you will likely dismiss your previous successes and doomed yourself to be a failure.

An unhappy client or a report with a spelling mistake would have disastrous consequences for you because you would be taking this personally; feeling upset after spending such a long time to make it perfect and still not getting it right would lead to frustration and anger.

Personal appearance: This is also one of the common areas of perfectionism that causes worry about how you look and dress. You may find that you spend a lot of time trying to find the right clothing for a social event, then still feel anxious because you worry that it may not be the perfect outfit for the occasion anyway.

Sports, physical activity: You may find yourself constantly checking the timing of your performance and of others, often comparing and perhaps even despairing.

Intimate relationships and friendships: Going out of your way, making many sacrifices to be the best friend, the best partner, and worrying when other friends meet up more or call each other more than they contact you.

Your expectations may also be high from them, and sometimes, it is hard for others to live up to those relentlessly high standards. The relentlessly high standards of a perfectionist can have a strain on all types of relationships.

Speaking and writing: You may believe that you must write perfectly with no mistakes and speak perfectly well, or people will judge you.

Housework/cleaning: You might feel stressed or even anxious if your home is not always tidy and immaculate. You may end up doing all the cleaning and tidying yourself because others may not do it up to your standards and fearing that friends coming to your home may judge you if it is not orderly and clean is also a part of this area.

Parenting: I think many mums can recognise this. The worry is that no matter what you do, you may not be doing a good enough job as a parent. This also comes with the fear that if you are not doing the perfect job as a parent, you might be responsible and damage your child's psychology and future somehow.

Social occasions: I often hear my clients saying, *"I worry that I may not have interesting enough things to say, and they may think I am boring"*. So there is this sense that we are responsible for entertaining everyone so the others really enjoy your company, or simply being the best host for your guests.

Health: You might like to make sure you eat healthy, which in itself is a good thing; however, it can start putting strain on your body and mind if you become rigid about every single thing, the number of calories, type of nutrition in much detail.

Decision-making: This type of perfectionism can be quite paralysing because of the fear of making a wrong decision and the consequences that it may bring. They say, *"Any decision is better than no decision."*

Perfectionism and other issues

Worry and anxiety: If you are living with perfectionism, you might likely have many future worries. You would find uncertainty hard to tolerate and want to know the best outcome for every decision you make. This may cause spending a lot of time procrastinating, trying to find possible outcomes, and thinking it may all go wrong and, as a result, cause prolonged stress and anxiety.

Obsessive Compulsive Disorder (OCD): You may be concerned about writing the perfect email or report so the person reading it does not doubt what you are trying to convey. This can result in reading it over and over again, and you may lose yourself in details, spending a lot more time than necessary and not being sure about whether it is good enough. This will, in the long term, cause burnout. The work will start piling up, causing you to stress and have a negative effect on your confidence. You may also find yourself having things in perfect order, cleanness and/or symmetry, spending a lot of time to reach the perfect level with the fear of consequences.

Social anxiety: The belief that others may judge you harshly about not being perfectly dressed or how you act or talk. The fear of being unable to make perfectly interesting conversations to entertain others can cause social anxiety, hindering you from attending social situations or being anxious when you make it to social gatherings.

Eating problems: You might like to keep rigid standards about your weight and your body at the perfect level for your set standards. This can easily lead to a desire to control what you are eating, which can result in eating problems in the long run.

Imposter syndrome: Perfectionism and Imposter Syndrome often go hand in hand. Constantly striving for flawlessness creates a breeding ground for imposter syndrome, where you believe your achievements are undeserved or you are somehow *"faking"* your competence. You may attribute your accomplishments to luck or external factors, completely dismissing your own skills and abilities. The fear of being exposed as a fraud intensifies the pressure to constantly prove yourself, preserving the cycle of perfectionism and reinforcing imposter syndrome.

Do any of these areas resonate with you? Let's first explore and understand what kind of areas might exactly be affecting you negatively. I would like you to take a moment and think about the areas that are affected by your relentlessly rigid high standards or the standards that you believe others are expecting of you.

So, there you have it - a basic overview of perfectionism and how it can affect your life. If you are struggling with perfectionism, please don't suffer in silence. Reach out for help and remember that you are not alone.

Have a look at the sheet on page 20 and start identifying your own perfectionism areas. You may also think of some situations that may have been related to your perfectionist tendencies, which you can put on the **"My Perfectionist Areas Sheet"**.

> **Being happy doesn't mean that everything is perfect.
> It means that you've decided to look beyond the imperfections.**
> - Gerard Way

You can download free ebooks, worksheets, audio-guided meditation and attention training at https://www.mindandmood.co.uk/resources/

Write down when you notice your perfectionism is getting in the way. It will help you gain more awareness of the specific areas.

My Perfectionist Areas Sheet

Areas of my perfectionism	Self-oriented, other-oriented, or socially prescribed
Example: Work, when I write emails.	Socially prescribed – In my position they would expect me to have the perfect writing skills and they will judge if I make spelling mistakes.
Example: Home, decision making.	Self-oriented – I cannot decide because I have to make the best decision, or it might have awful consequences on myself and my family.

Chapter 2

Ready for a Shift? Pinpointing Change

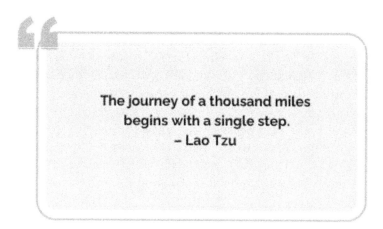

**The journey of a thousand miles
begins with a single step.
– Lao Tzu**

If you bought this book and came as far as this page, it probably means that you are having the negative impacts of your perfectionist thoughts, emotions and behaviour in your life and would like to work on making some changes.

This is a fantastic first step towards your better future self. It takes bravery and determination to be able to take the first single step because once you have taken that step, it means you are opening your mind to personal growth and a more flexible outlook in life.

Change is possible if the pain you are experiencing right now is greater than the effort you will have to put in to change.

Take a few minutes to think about what you would like to get out of reading this book, what you would like to achieve and why. Sometimes, we give up achieving a goal because we try to get there too quickly or by doing everything at once, which becomes overwhelming.

Think about losing weight, for example, if you diet vigorously, trying to lose a lot of weight within a week or two, you are quite likely to give up. When we want something, we often want to get there quickly. It is hard to wait, right?

Change is not easy because we subconsciously try to avoid the unknown. What we are used to is what we know, and our brain is wired to feel safe with what we know, even sometimes when we know it is not good for us.

Giving up or delaying something before you even start because you are not doing it perfectly is also a typical perfectionist trait. For example, giving up learning how to play the piano because you are not doing it perfectly or not speaking a foreign language you have learned.

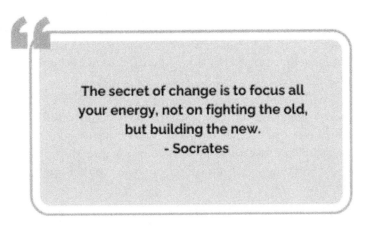

> The secret of change is to focus all your energy, not on fighting the old, but building the new.
> - Socrates

Another important thing about change is to be okay with setbacks, but each setback provides learning, which we can reflect upon and helps us move forward with the change we want to make.

What is your ideal self like? How are you thinking, feeling, and behaving differently, and where are you? Who are you with when you have achieved your goals? In terms of taking action, it's important that we first decide our goals. What do you want to achieve?

When you focus on worry, your energy flows towards worry, and the worry grows, and when you concentrate on calm gratitude, your energy flows towards it and changes the way you feel. Be careful where you turn the focus of your attention. In the free resources I am offering, you can download **"Attention Training Audio"**, which will help your mind focus on where you want to focus.

I heard a story about a white-water rafting trainer. When he first started as a trainer, he used to tell the students to watch out for the rock or watch out for the tree truck, and sure enough, all the students would turn towards the obstacle and hit it. This taught the trainer not to draw students' attention to what to avoid but to focus on the direction that they should be going. He started pointing, *"Everyone this way!"* and the whole team would focus on the direction that would keep them going.

Fill in the **"My Supercharging Change"** sheet to start with. Write down where you are right now and how your perfectionism affects you and those around you. Have you had enough of this? Is the pain greater than the effort you have to put in to make the changes?

Now start moving your focus on how you want to reclaim your life and what is the story you want to write for your future and why. Your past does not define you. This part about the change you want to make is really important; make sure that you can connect with the deepest reason why you want to make this change.

Maybe you are tired of feeling down, feeling like a victim, others making decisions for you, and never standing up for yourself. Or perhaps you are tired of the negative chatter in your head, telling you others are better than you are, and no matter how hard you try, you are never quite there.

Your motivation to achieve your goal is really important. Why do you want to make a change? Is it because you want better health, more headspace, more time for yourself, your family and so on? Whatever change you want to make, just think about why you desire to do this.

Now, visualise it. It is extremely powerful to visualise because our mind does not know whether we are really there or just imagining that we are there. This is also the reason why we can get anxious just by imagining something bad might be happening.

Use this power your mind has to your advantage and start imagining the positive changes. Your mind will start believing you are there and help you get there; notice the opportunities to get you there as well.

Now, just take a moment to lean back, close your eyes if you like and give yourself a few moments to visualise what it would look like once you have achieved this change. Think about how it will feel like, what you will be doing, where you will be, and whom you will be with when you have achieved this goal after you have made this lasting change.

Also, just notice if there is any avoidance. Could it be too complex, or is your goal too overwhelming, which may get you into freeze mode? You know about the deer that freezes in the middle of the road with headlights? Did you freeze because it's just too much and too complicated?

Remember, you just need to take one step at a time to get to the top of the mountain.

In order to make these small steps clearer, it would be helpful to break the goals down into smaller tasks, which would be **Specific, Measurable, Achievable, Realistic, and Time-based.**

Let's say you set a goal of *"spending more time with my family"*, but this is too broad and vague. You can say I will spend 1 hour twice a week with my children for the next four weeks to play games, read stories, go for walks or parks together as a family, and so on. Remember to think about "why" you want to do this and why it is important for you.

My "Supercharging Change" Sheet

Things I would like to change.	How are they serving me right now?	What I want.	My reasons why I want to achieve this.	The first step I will take towards my goal.			
Feeling anxious when I go to a social gathering.	Not good. Sometimes I decline invitations, because I worry that I will not be able to keep making intelligent and fun conversations all the time, and people will think I am boring.	Feel more confident and relaxed in social situations and be able to talk to people without worrying what they will think about me.	Because I want to be able to enjoy and have fun when I am out rather than worry and be anxious.	I will accept the invitation to my friend's birthday party next weekend, I know many of the people, with others I will practice the mindset that " I am unique and interesting" .			

"

**If you always do what you've always done,
you'll always get what you've always got.
- Henry Ford**

Now that you are clear about what areas of perfectionism are negatively affecting your life, the reasons why you desire to make changes, and how you can take smaller steps in order to achieve the bigger changes, we can have a look at the challenges you may encounter and the resources you have that will help you overcome these challenges.

Work on peeling the challenges layer by layer to get to the bottom of your real fear. One important thing to remember about **"FEAR"** is that it is what is limiting you and holding you back from getting what you want:

False
Evidence
Appearing
Real

Is there really a physical barrier that is stopping you from what you want, or is it about the fears? We will look at the ways to challenge the limiting beliefs in the coming chapters.

Now, it is time to have some more structure on your steps towards what you want and how you want to shape your future. Think of both internal and external resources. The people that could help and support you to get to where you want to be, all the external resources you can use, and what kind of personal qualities and strengths you have internally.

I have put an example on the **"My Challenges and Resources"** sheet; you can then personalise the sheet in accordance with your goals, challenges, fears and resources. This is a great start to the journey towards your inner world and the limiting beliefs that are holding you back without being questioned.

"My Challenges and Resources" Sheet

The challenges and the obstacles that may get in my way	My internal and external resources to overcome the challenges
A new project at work may mean that I have to work day and night to complete it, and I will not have any time to spend with my children as I had planned. Why: I must finish the project to make sure it is perfectly done Why: Otherwise, we may lose the client if they don't like it, and then I might get the blame and lose my job. FEAR: Failure! I will not have enough money to pay the mortgage and give my family what they deserve. All my family will be ashamed of me.	**Inner resources:** I have managed to say "no" before, and I can negotiate the deadline, so I do not have to work until late at night. Time with my children is important to me, and I want them to remember the quality time we spend together. I have determination and love for my children as an inner strength that will help me overcome the challenges. **External resources:** My boss is actually quite understanding and believes in family/work balance. I can ask for others' help and delegate some of the work. I don't have to do it all alone. I can ask my husband to help me out with this goal by reminding me why I wanted to make this change in the first place.

Top tips

- There is a difference between setting high standards but when you don't reach them, taking the learning onboard for personal growth – and the relentlessly high standards that take all your energy, all the time leaving you upset, disappointed, sad, angry, and you constantly pay a high price to reach them.

- You might have learned that perfectionism is a good thing through modelling, rigid and high standards from your parents and positive reinforcement such as promotions, pay rises, etc. Genetics can also play a part in developing perfectionist tendencies.

- It is okay to have personal goals in life; however, when the bar is constantly set higher, the goals become harder and harder to achieve.

- You may have self-oriented, other-oriented or socially prescribed perfectionism or all three, and these may come up in different areas of your life. Just notice first and observe the type or types of perfectionism that might be causing you distress. Change starts with gaining awareness and getting to know yourself.

> "
>
> The curious paradox is that when I accept
> myself as I am, then I can change.
> – Carl Rogers

Let's Explore Perfectionism in the Cognitive Behavioural Way

I would like to look at perfectionism from the CBT (Cognitive Behavioural Therapy) perspective. In the following chapters, we will dive deep into the type of thoughts and beliefs, emotions, physical sensations and behaviour of perfectionists in much more detail. However, I would like to emphasise that I have always intended this book to be a light reading, so I will not be going into all the textbook/academic details of all history, formulations and references etc. of CBT, just a quick explanation of main principles in order to make sense of the connections.

CBT assumes that a person's perception of a situation - formed by their early experiences - can trigger irrational thoughts and blocking beliefs, which directly affect the emotions, physical sensations and how they respond to that situation. The formulation for CBT was referred to as *"hot cross bun"* for the first time by Christine Padesky, and it looks exactly like that.

For example, my client Amy's parents were both successful solicitors and have always been expecting Amy to do well in life. Amy had to work all through her childhood to receive praise and affection from both her parents.

She learned that she received this when she did something extremely well or got the highest marks in school and got into the university her parents hoped she would. There may also be some genetic components that can be harder to pinpoint exactly. For Amy, there was nothing in between the highest mark or else fail, get the job she applied for, or else a failure.

Amy also held high standards in her intimate relationship about how often her boyfriend should call and what he must do; either it had to be perfect, or she became stressed that they were failing. She has also been working very hard to be the perfect girlfriend and to show others that they had the perfect relationship with the perfect home, the perfect garden, the perfect furniture and so on.

When Amy's long-term relationship ended, her formulation looked as below.

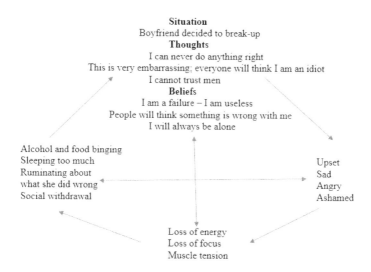

Christine Padesky's Cognitive Behavioural Cycle (Hot Cross Bun)

This is the vicious cycle, and the content may change, but the process remains the same unless the unhelpful beliefs one day are reviewed, challenged, replaced and practised in more helpful ways to pursue a more fulfilling life, which gives the person a sense of self-worth from inside through strategies rather than evaluating yourself with your unrealistically high standards, which we will be looking at in this book in the coming chapters.

My short formulation below has been helping my clients facilitate change towards a thriving life.

In order to start using the formulation, we need to gain awareness into what is happening inside of us, and what kind of reaction it results with. How do we behave in order to cope with our triggers, or do we employ avoidance strategies?

I would like to emphasise that language is everything; it is how we make sense of the world around us as well as inside of us. Brené Brown talked about a research they conducted with 7000 people, asking what emotions they could identify clearly, and most people could only identify three emotions: Happy, Sad and Mad.

When feelings are triggered, it can be hard to be able to express them, possibly because our logical brain is much younger than the emotional brain. We may have a mayhem of emotions happening inside without being able to express them clearly, and of course, this causes deep frustration, and we may even end up lashing out because often anger is a masking emotion, overriding sadness.

Change takes insight. It takes awareness and meaningful reason. Why do I want to change? What's the reason that I want to make this change? It's normal to have a setback. What matters is learning from it to grow and move forwards towards how you want your life to be.

Working on making change is an upward spiral; you learn from and grow with every setback. There's perfection in being real, just being you with your strengths and your shortcomings. There are 7.9 billion other people on Earth: there's only one of you. You are unique.

Change takes insight, awareness, a meaningful reason, repetition, time, and willingness.

STAGES OF CHANGE

PRE-CONTEMPLATION
No intention to changing behaviour

CONTEMPLATION
Aware that a problem exists, but no commitment to take actoin yet

RELAPSE
Fall beck into old patterns of behaviour

UPWARD SPIRAL
Learn from each relapse

PREPARATION
Intend on taking action to address the problem

MAINTENANCE
Sustained change, new behaviour replacing the old

ACTION
Active modification on the problem behaviour

Prochaska & DiClemente, 1984

Top tips:

It is normal to have a setback. What matters is to learn from it to move forwards towards how you want your life to be.

There is perfection in being real, being *"you"* with your strengths and shortcomings, just like the other 7.9 billion people on earth. There is only one *"you"*, which makes you unique.

Self-acceptance is one of the biggest steps towards a happier and more fulfilling life. Be *"mindful"*, be in today, at this very moment, and pay attention to things you get right and count your blessings. Once you set your intention in the morning, the filtering system in your brain will help you notice information that you have dismissed before, and it can be life changing.

Choose to be "kind to yourself" and choose the direction you would like to steer your life towards.

> **The most beautiful and profound way to change yourself is to accept yourself completely, as imperfect as you are.**
> **– Maxime Lagacé**

Now, let's explore what you feel about some situations that you find causing negative thoughts and emotions and look at how you handle them. Just make notes of the latest event that you can think of that caused you distress and perhaps resulted in unhelpful behaviour.

Exploring the Maintenance Cycle

Situation (What happened)	Thoughts	Emotions	Behaviour

There is also a Cognitive Behavioural Model of Perfectionism by Shafran and colleagues (2010), in which they explore the cognitive and behavioural principles that keep perfectionism going. Let's explore it the model with performance related perfectionism.

Model of Perfectionism

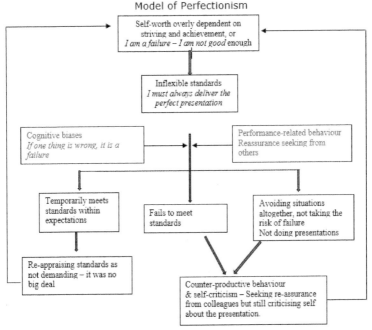

Shafran and colleagues (2010)

In this model of perfectionism by Shafran et al. (2010), self-worth depends on achieving high and inflexible standards as a central principle. Let's have an overview of how the model addresses the consequences of failing to meet those standards, the role of avoidance, and the cycle created when temporarily meeting standards:

-Self-worth and high inflexible standards: Perfectionists often tie their sense of self-worth to their ability to meet excessively high and rigid standards. They believe that their worth as a person is contingent upon achieving perfection in various domains of life, such as work, appearance, or relationships, which we looked at in further detail in Chapter 1. This core belief sets the stage for the emotional and behavioural responses associated with perfectionism. The performance-related behaviour can very well be a presentation, staying till late at work, spending too many hours checking your work, trying to be the best entertainer in a social situation and so on.

-Consequences of failing to meet standards: When perfectionists perceive themselves as falling short of their high standards, for example, making a mistake on a report, they tend to experience intense self-criticism, feelings of shame, and a diminished sense of self-worth. Failing to meet their own expectations can trigger negative emotions like anxiety, sadness, or frustration. These emotional reactions further reinforce the belief that anything less than perfection is unacceptable.

-Avoidance: In response to the fear of failure, criticism, or not measuring up to their standards, perfectionists often engage in various forms of avoidance. This can include avoiding tasks or situations where they anticipate potential failure, procrastinating to delay potential evaluation, or seeking constant reassurance from others to alleviate anxiety. Avoidance behaviours provide temporary relief from distress but contribute to maintaining the perfectionistic cycle.

-Temporary achievement of standards: On occasion, perfectionists may temporarily meet their high standards and receive external validation or recognition for their achievements. While this can provide a sense of relief and accomplishment, it often doesn't last long.

-Re-appraising standards as insufficiently demanding: Once they occasionally reach their extremely high standards, perfectionists may quickly dismiss the achievement as no big deal, anyone could have done it, and shift their focus to new and even higher standards, striving for continuous perfection and fearing that their past achievements are not sufficient. This perpetuates the cycle of setting unattainable goals and feeling inadequate when those goals are not met consistently.

You can see that the cycle of perfectionism involves a continuous loop of setting unrealistically high standards, experiencing distress when those standards are not met, engaging in avoidance strategies to cope with the anxiety, and temporarily feeling relief when standards are temporarily achieved. However, the relief is short-lived, as the cycle repeats with new standards, perpetuating the unattainable quest for perfection.

In the coming chapters, we will explore the type of thoughts, limiting beliefs, emotions and behaviour connected to perfectionism and make more sense of the CBT formulation. We will also start working on having more awareness of those beliefs, emotions and behaviour so you can recognise them when it is happening and take a distance to challenge whether those beliefs are facts or just strongly held opinions.

I will guide you step by step to challenge and modify your perfectionistic beliefs, develop more flexible standards, and reduce the reliance on external validation for your self-worth. By addressing avoidance behaviours, developing healthier coping strategies, and fostering self-compassion, you can break free from the perfectionistic cycle and cultivate a more balanced and fulfilling approach to life.

You can download free ebooks, worksheets, audio-guided meditation and attention training at https://www.mindandmood.co.uk/resources/

Chapter 3

Brainpower Explored:
Understanding Our Control Centre

> Your beliefs become your thoughts,
> Your thoughts become your words,
> Your words become your actions,
> Your actions become your habits,
> Your habits become your values,
> Your values become your destiny.
> - Mahatma Gandhi

Let's continue from the previous chapter about the basis of Cognitive Behavioural Therapy. The *"mind, body, emotions and behaviour"* are undeniably connected and constantly affect each other, so it would not make complete sense to look into one and not the others. I would like to start by looking at the engine room, the mainframe where everything happens behind the scenes: *"The incredible brain"*.

During my years at the university studying Psychology, I was always extremely fascinated by the brain and the fMRI (Functional Magnetic Resonance Imaging) scans, which are used to monitor the areas of brain activity by looking at the blood flow to different parts of the brain.

I am certainly not an expert in neuroscience; however, I guess we can all agree in a simplistic way that the brain's language is electricity. The neural communication is provided by the electrical impulses releasing neurotransmitters between the synapsis, which underpin each and every thought, emotion and action we experience. Those neural connections are what create *"the mind"*.

After the first few articles were published about brain activity and fMRI scans in the 1990s, the studies in this area have drastically increased to understand the patterns in our brain in relation to our thoughts, perceptions, memory, actions and emotions.

Not long ago, they used to believe that *"Pathways in our brain are set, we cannot change"*; however, thanks to fMRI technology, we know now that our brains have neuroplasticity. More so when we are children, but also when we are adults, which is great news! It means we have the possibility to change our ways if they are no longer serving us for a happy and fulfilling life.

Our amazing brain creates the mind, the experience of our existence. Of how the pathways work, how different parts of our brain have different responsibilities and that they all work only for one thing: The survival of the individual. Just a basic understanding of these can help you take control of your present and your future.

The past is past, and it does not define you. Make a conscious decision to let go of it rather than wasting your precious brainpower on things you cannot change. Learn where there are lessons to be learned and move on.

Parts of the brain. *Not all, just the ones we are interested in.*

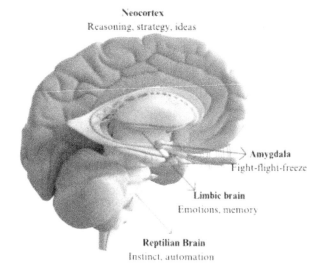

The three parts of the brain

Let's first see what is happening in this book's relevant parts. There are three major parts. I will reiterate that this is really rough because I think any neurologist would be completely horrified by my statement. However, this is just to explain in a very simple way what happens and in which part of the brain so we can look at how thinking, feeling, physical sensations and behaviour are closely connected.

The youngest part of our human brain is the "Neocortex", about 2-3 million years old. This is really what differentiates us from other species. The closest species to humans are chimpanzees, and considering the DNA sequence between the two species is apparently 99% identical, they must really feel cheated. Or perhaps we could have been happier if we hung around and not had a care in the world about the past or the future.

The neocortex is the area of logical thinking, decision-making, memory, attention, reflection, and awareness. It helps us look at the past, put it together with the present time and project into the future. This is the rational part of our brain, and because it is also the youngest, it is quite slow compared to other parts.

The reptilian brain is the oldest part of our human brain, over 350 million years old. The autonomic nervous system in this part is responsible for all automatic functions such as breathing, heartbeat, digestive system, liver functions, etc., so we don't have to think about starting the digestive system after we eat; it just happens automatically. That is pretty good, so we don't have to use brainpower to remember to keep the digestive system going or tell ourselves to breathe or heart to beat.

Emotions storage – *The home of anxiety and panic*

Our limbic brain is the part that stores emotionally attached memories (happy, sad, scary, etc.), and most importantly, the *"amygdala"* in this part of the brain, is responsible for the survival response: fight, flight or freeze. This was specifically useful when we as humans were living in caves, going out hunting and had to be very aware of dangers around us.

It is also useful if we are in the woods and under attack by let's say, a bear or just about to walk in front of a moving car while daydreaming. When there is a threat, the eyes or ears or both send signals to the amygdala, which interprets the sounds and images.

Interestingly, we don't have to be physically in a situation for the brain activity to happen. Researchers found that even by imagining a scenario, the participants' brain activity showed activity in the regions in accordance with their personality traits *(Hassabis et. Al. "Imagine All the People: How the Brain*

Creates and Uses Personality Models to Predict Behavior". Cerebral Cortex, 2013; DOI: 10.1093/cercor/bht042).

This becomes complicated when we start thinking that something bad might happen in the future and lies in the basis of why we suffer from anxiety when, in fact, nothing dangerous is happening around us. But what is happening in our brain/mind is a different story.

When we perceive something bad might happen, the amygdala perceives danger just by thinking about it or imagining it. The amygdala instantly sends stress signals to the hypothalamus, which is like a "control centre" that communicates with the autonomic nervous system to trigger fight, flight or freeze responses.

You can imagine if those were friends, it would be similar to Eric, Dave and friends (information coming through eyes, ears and other senses) giving Adam (amygdala) a call, saying, *"Hey, we need you man, we are in danger",* and Adam says *"Erhhm let me see if that really is the case",* once convinced, Adam shouts at Henry (hypothalamus) *"Hey Henry gather the troops, we are in danger. Don't ask questions; do as I say! Just send the troops man!"* So, Henry presses the button to depart all the troops. *"All systems go"* and sets a series of automatic physiological responses in our body, preparing for survival.

What happens when the survival system is activated?
Hell of a lot happens in the body!

- Rapid breathing in order to get more oxygen into the system to power the muscles.
- Faster heart rate to pump the blood to larger muscles.
- Release adrenaline and cortisol.
- Tunnel vision in order to focus on the threat or the escape way.

- Sweaty palms in order to keep the system cool.
- Blood diversion from the digestive system to the muscles where it is more needed because your survival is more imperative than digesting your food. This can feel like knots in your stomach.
- Dry mouth as the digestive system shuts down.

It is a real miracle that all of this just happens non-voluntary as soon as the brain perceives danger. The sympathetic nervous system controls the body's fight-or-flight response, producing a rapid, unconscious, automatic reaction.

The other day, as I was driving down the lane, a squirrel came running from the side of the road, and I found myself hitting the break instantly and unaware of being near death; the squirrel continued with his happy jump with its dancing like tail to the other side of the road.

What happened to me was a completely different story. I noticed my shaking hands, my heart beating so fast that it felt like it could almost jump out of my chest, and my stomach felt like it had turned inwards. I just thought, *"Wow, what a miracle that my brain activated all these response systems in a split second, and it all happened without me even thinking about it. If I had time to think, the poor squirrel would have been flat dead in the road"*.

The amygdala and hypothalamus are so effectively wired that all of the above happens before the neocortex has even had a chance to process what was happening. The neocortex is more like Glen, who shows up after the fight and says, *"Oh my, looks like that was close!"*. Because the thinking happens after the response, this is also called *"Amygdala hijack"*.

Real vs. perceived danger: Anxiety!

Unfortunately, this part of our brain is simply not quite ready for 21ˢᵗ-century living and the pressure. It is all really good and useful that we have a great system to protect ourselves; however, the problem occurs when we are not in real danger but perceive that something bad might happen.

Our brain does not know whether we are in real danger or just imagining what might happen, so we find ourselves in a state of stress, sometimes panic and in certain situations, cannot even think clearly due to *"Amygdala highjack"*.

Perhaps a project deadline, a presentation, friends coming for dinner that we want to impress, or a wedding we are invited to can trigger negative thoughts and a series of stress hormones, resulting in physical sensations and unhelpful behaviour, such as avoidance.

What you practice grows stronger

About 86 billion neurons are forming 100 trillion connections to each other to help us function. That's a lot of neurons! When we are learning, the neurons start firing to make a pathway together and even though in the beginning, it feels hard, with practice, they become automatic.

You may not remember how you learned to walk, but you no longer have to focus on it; you just walk. Or if you are learning how to play an instrument, you make strange and sometimes unbearable noises until you have practised a song so many times that it becomes fluent, similar to driving, learning dancing or a new language.

This very same thing goes also for the way we think. When we begin forming ideas about ourselves, others and the world around us, these neurons start firing together, building the pathways of beliefs. And because we are all unique and our experiences of the world around us and ourselves are different, mixed with genetics, we all see the world differently.

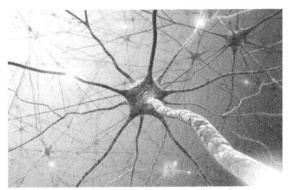

Neurons that fire together wire together.

If you drive, you may remember what it was like the first time you sat by the wheel to learn how to drive. It can be really confusing, and there are so many things to coordinate, right? Check the mirrors, start the car, clutch down the first gear, hand break down, slowly give gas, take your foot off the clutch, and so on. And the first few times, the car may come to a halt, and you try again. If you have been driving for a while, you probably don't even think about these anymore.

I bet you just get in the car and drive off now. It is the same way when we learn to dance, play an instrument, learn a new language, and learn about the world, others, and ourselves. The more we practice, the more automatic it becomes.

For many years, it has been believed that a person's way was set in stone and could not be changed, hence the old belief: *"The pathways are set and cannot be changed"*. However, as technology advances, *research shows that the brain has neuroplasticity. It is possible to see and do things differently by changing our perspective, which no longer serves us.*

Neural pathways in a nutshell

Strong neural pathway
(What you practice)

Weak neural pathway
(New learning)

A great example of that is Destin Sandlin, who is a mechanic. One day, his friend changed the mechanics of his bike as a joke: if the handle turned right, the wheels would turn left, and vice versa, the exact opposite of a normal bike.

Destin was determined to work this out and thought, how difficult can this be? It took him about 8 months to learn to ride the backwards bike, but he got there and was able to ride comfortably. The pathways in his brain for the normal bike had weakened, and new pathways were formed.

However, his 6 years old son cracked this in a couple of hours, which shows that children have higher neuroplasticity than adults, but we as adults can still change our ways. It just takes more practice.

Destin wanted to go back to riding an ordinary bike again and had to spend some time to be able to do so. Any small distraction would throw him back to old ways; if his phone rang, he would lose his balance, but eventually, the usual way of cycling became natural for him again. You can watch this interesting experience on the below link.

https://www.youtube.com/watch?v=MFzDaBzBlL0

Amazingly, our thoughts and beliefs are exactly the same way as we learn to do anything else. Driving, dancing, playing an instrument, and thinking are all built the same way in the brain. The neurons travelling between the same synapsis make stronger pathways and even shortcuts, so what we think, believe, feel and do becomes *automatic*.

You might have heard of Pavlov's dogs. Pavlov kept ringing a bell before feeding the dogs, then realised that the dogs were salivating as soon as they heard the bell before they even saw the food. The dogs were conditioned to anticipate food when they heard the bell, and a strong learning pathway was built. Pavlov then wanted to see if this could be undone, and sure enough, when the bell rang and there was no food, the dogs stopped salivating after a while.

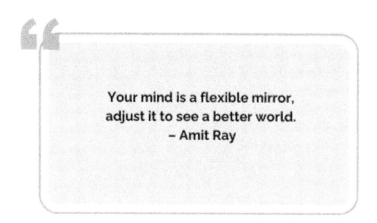

> **Your mind is a flexible mirror,**
> **adjust it to see a better world.**
> **– Amit Ray**

As you can see from the scientifically proven examples above, we can learn to do things differently, think differently, and look at the world differently. Yes, it is easy to fall back into old habits when we get distracted, and it takes extra effort to change old habits with new and more helpful ones; however, it is certainly possible. This proves that we are not just set rigidly in our ways and *"we can change if we set our mind to it".*

Reticular Activating System - RAS

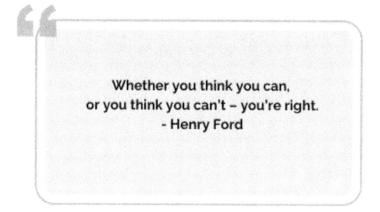

> **Whether you think you can,**
> **or you think you can't – you're right.**
> **– Henry Ford**

This famous quote by Henry Ford underlines the importance of attitude in determining success or failure.

The Reticular Activating System (RAS) is also what I call the "magic system" that works for *"you"*. It constantly tries to prove you right, so it filters the information according to your beliefs about the world and what matters to you.

This system, which consists physically of a bundle of nerves in our brainstem, has an important responsibility. Our brains are amazing processors; however, we are bombarded with millions and billions of types of information all day long. We would simply short-circuit if they were all allowed through to our brain. RAS filters only the information that is important to us according to our beliefs and values.

You may have several eyewitnesses to the same crime, and you will get many different statements from them. Why is that? Because they have all filtered the information that mattered to them. You may decide to buy a new car, and let's say you have chosen a blue Toyota Yaris; you will start noticing all the blue Toyota Yaris' that are driving on the roads. Why? Because it suddenly has a meaning to you, it is your new car, you may be paying attention to what kind of people are driving them, how they look on the road.

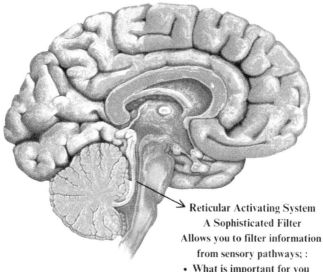

Reticular Activating System
A Sophisticated Filter
Allows you to filter information
from sensory pathways; :
- **What is important for you**
- **Supports your beliefs**
- **Keeps out what doesn't matter**

If you believe that you are a failure unless you deliver the perfect report, your RAS will filter in that one mistake you have made. If you believe you are not lovable, RAS will filter in all the information to prove you are right. RAS does not have its own mind. It just does its job to prove you right.

For perfectionists, it will become the selective attention to failure rather than their achievements. But here is the great news: we know that our brains have neuroplasticity and that we can challenge and replace our beliefs. That means that if you decide to change your mindset to, for example, *"I am lovable"*, *"I am worthy,"* or/and "I am good enough exactly as I am", at first, the switch may need effort, but after a while, you will realise that your RAS will start working toward proving that you are right.

So go on, start working on challenging and changing your unhelpful beliefs today, and start noticing the things you have been dismissing.

Top tips:

- All activity and communication in the brain happen through electrical impulses when the neurotransmitters release chemicals at synapsis. The more they travel on the same pathway, the stronger the pathway becomes.
- This is how we learn "everything"! Walking, talking, thinking, behaving. The more we do it, the more habitual it becomes. For example, the more you worry, the better you become at worrying.
- It is possible to change our thinking and behavioural habits if they no longer serve us.
- You can use your R.A.S. system to help you notice the information you have dismissed and find evidence to prove your new, positive mindset!

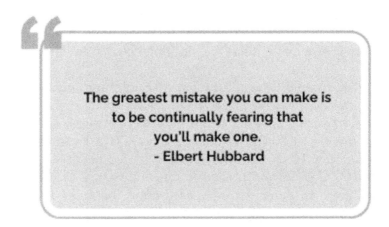

The greatest mistake you can make is
to be continually fearing that
you'll make one.
- Elbert Hubbard

Chapter 4

Decoding Perfectionist Thoughts and Beliefs

In order to make changes to the ways that we think, feel and act/react, we need to understand exactly what is not serving us. This is the part of the self-discovery journey, an important part because we are going to look at the cognitive part of CBT.

You saw in the previous chapter how thoughts are made. We start learning about the world, ourselves and others at very early ages in order to make sense of the world, where we stand as an individual, where others stand and what kind of a place the world is.

Do you recognise any of the following statements?

- I must always deliver perfect results.
- I must never make mistakes.
- It's my fault if things are not right.
- I don't trust others to do as good a job as I do, so I end up doing it all.
- I am not good enough.
- I must cook the perfect meal for my guests; otherwise, they won't come again.
- If I don't dress perfectly right for the occasion, people will laugh at me.
- If I am overweight, I am not good enough.

The power of words

We make sense of the world through language. All day long and even at night, you are listening to yourself. The thoughts keep flying around in your mind, and sometimes, you may find this constant negative chatter in your mind.

We are born pure, free from all judgements, prejudice, opinions, and beliefs. Our minds are just pure and clean. Recent research shows that the brain of a foetus starts showing electrical activity from about week 7. In the third trimester, the cerebral cortex starts to take over from the brain stem, preparing the baby for future learning and development. From the moment we are born, our brain is like a sponge, taking in everything happening around us.

Apart from learning how to eat, crawl, walk, talk and so on, we start forming ideas about ourselves, others and the world. Some of those are positive, i.e... *"I am intelligent, I am good at this, I make mummy laugh,"* etc. some are neutral, and some are negative.

If you have heard or thought enough times that the world is a dangerous place, bad things always happen to you or your family, good things always happen to others, you can never do anything right, other people's children are doing better, get praise only when you bring home best marks, your view of the world will start building around this information.

You will likely start believing other people are better than you, good things never happen to you, you must always get the best result in anything, and nothing else is good enough. Often, these beliefs go unchallenged into our adulthood.

We have looked at the pathways earlier, and the more we think in a certain way, the stronger the pathways become, so the thoughts become automatic like reflexes and can be easily triggered in certain situations.

How we speak to ourselves and communicate with ourselves matters because it creates and shapes our world and how we live our lives.

Look at the below *Unhelpful Thinking Habits* and see if you recognise any of them in your own thinking patterns. The first step is to pause, be mindful and recognise when you have these thoughts. Once we understand the types of unhelpful thinking habits and which ones we use the most, we will start challenging them by looking for evidence for and against them.

Unhelpful thinking habits

Mind reading

This is a very typical thinking style, especially when you assume you know what others are thinking, especially about you and certain situations. If you are a perfectionist, you might find yourself believing that others are harshly judgemental in their ways and they think you are not good enough.

They think I am stupid.
They think I don't deserve to be here.
They are all hoping that I will fail.
They won't think my house is tidy.
Others will judge me if I don't do everything perfectly (i.e. My house, my job, my cooking, my clothes).
They think I am an idiot for not giving the correct answer.
My parents think I am a failure for not getting the promotion.
People think I am not good enough to handle this.

Labelling

You might find yourself focusing on the things you did not do as well as you wanted to do or the decisions that turned out to be less favourable and find yourself putting yourself down, blaming yourself for things that may not even be your responsibility.

I am useless.
I am not good enough.
I am such an idiot.
I should never have made that decision.
I am such an idiot for not knowing the answer to a simple question.
People are so stupid.

All-or-nothing/Black-or-white thinking

Always focusing on the best outcome that you must achieve; all else is a fail. There is never a grey zone, so that the thinking style would be very rigid.

If I don't get the job I applied for, I am a failure.
I must always resolve everything.
All clients must always be happy with my reports.
Everyone must like me.

Underestimating achievements

This is quite a common way that perfectionists see their achievements. You may have been working very hard to achieve something, perhaps a new job or a big project; however, once it is done and you get praised, you will often find yourself saying;

"No big deal, anyone can do it", and setting the bar higher for next time.

Should and must – always and never

You might find yourself putting a lot of *"should and must"* and/or *"always and never"* into your sentences throughout the day. These words symbolise unrealistic demands and pressure on oneself, others or what you think of others' expectations of you.

I must never make mistakes.
They should have done a better job.
I must always give my friends a helping hand.
My house should always be immaculate.
I always call my friends, they never call me.
I must make interesting conversations in a social situation.

Catastrophising

Does blowing things out of proportion, even though the problem can be quite small, sound familiar? Imagining an event in the past or future will have an awful outcome, and you will not be able to cope with it.

I did not come up with ideas in the meeting; they will probably fire me
If I am not perfectly well-spoken, people will think I am not well-educated (mind reading) and will not want to be friends with me. (catastrophizing)

Prediction

You might be predicting what will happen in the future, making assumptions about how something will go.

Because I cannot make interesting conversations, no one will like me, and I will end up all alone for the rest of my life.
I will not get the promotion, and it will all go bad, they might fire me.

I will do badly in presentations/meetings, and people will laugh behind my back.

Unfair focus

Perfectionists usually dismiss their achievements, even though they would have been working hard for it. For example, you might have been working really hard and a long time to get your dream job, but when people congratulate you and say you did great, you are most likely to say.

"Ah, it's no big deal; anyone can do it".

On the other hand, when you do not get your dream job in the first interview, you will lose all belief in yourself, be extremely self-critical, and think.

"I am useless".
"Everyone thinks I am such a failure, and the fact that I did not get the job proves this".

Negatively self-focused comparison

Perfectionists are often very critical of themselves and notice others' successes. You might find yourself thinking.

"Others always get what they want; they are much more successful than I am; everyone did better than I did in the meeting".

What if?

This is a very common way of thinking for perfectionists. When you are a perfectionist, you almost want to be sure of everything and every possible outcome, so what if would be an attempt to cover all possible outcomes due to intolerance of uncertainty with the hope of trying to gain some kind of control over the outcome.

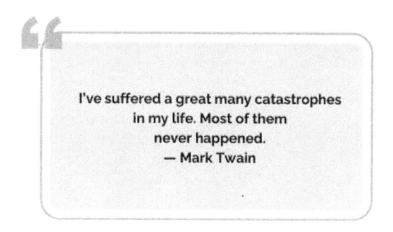

> I've suffered a great many catastrophes
> in my life. Most of them
> never happened.
> — Mark Twain

Always and never

Many of us find ourselves generalising events and people; however, as a perfectionist, you might often find yourself making generalised statements based on a single event.
Bad things always happen to me.
I can never trust others.
I never win; others are always luckier than I am.

Mental filter

Mental filter is a system in our brainstem that only focuses on the information we believe is true and important to us, i.e., noticing one mistake we made on a report and not paying attention that the rest is flawless.

Limiting beliefs

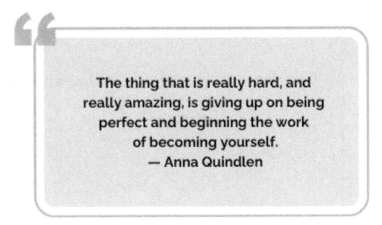

> The thing that is really hard, and really amazing, is giving up on being perfect and beginning the work of becoming yourself.
> — Anna Quindlen

What are beliefs and can they be changed? How come we all have different beliefs about ourselves, others and the world depending on our circumstances and our past? Are they facts or just our opinion?

Beliefs are the statements that we have about ourselves, the world and others. I am reliable, I am a good person, the world is a safe place, and others are kind. These are the sort of beliefs that we all like. Those beliefs make us feel good about ourselves, others and the world we live in.

The problem starts when we start hitting the bottom line of limiting beliefs.
I am not good enough.
I am boring.
I am a failure.
The world is unpredictable and dangerous.
Others are judgemental.
I am a bad person/friend.
I am not in control.
I am stupid.
I am boring.

These are some of the examples of the types of beliefs that cause us anxiety, stress and depression.

Our mind is like a tree

If you think about us, like a tree, we have automatic thoughts at the top. They are the branches, the leaves of the tree. These are relatively easy to see. You can detect your automatic thoughts much easier with a bit of awareness and being able to step back.

Those thoughts have been there for so long that they're automated, for example, your inner critique. You don't even realise you're thinking about them; you just feel the emotions very quickly.

Then we have the tree trunk, which is about the rules and assumptions. These are the should and musts, as well as if....

then.... sentences. They help us not to get down to the limiting beliefs, which are the tree's root. I must always help others. If I don't help others, then they may no longer like me.

The root of the tree represents our beliefs, which we learn mostly in the early years of our lives, the ideas about ourselves, about others, and the world. So, if you believe, for example, "I am not good enough or I am not as good as others", so you will employ some rules. If I never say no to work I am given, they will not notice that I'm not good enough".

We employ some rules to stay away from the negative and limiting beliefs. I am saying negative because they trigger *"fear"* and get in the way of things we are capable of doing. They stop us from taking chances, having the ability to relax, having fun, travelling, and even unlocking our full potential. *They steal our well-deserved happiness!*

The limiting beliefs take a bit of working on, but you can question them and change them. Suppose they are no longer serving you or helping you have a happy and fulfilling life. In that case, you can work with your RAS (Reticular Activating System), challenge limiting beliefs, find evidence for the opposite, break down the barriers and live a joyful life.

One way to test out and start questioning thoughts and limiting beliefs is to apply the principle of a court case to our beliefs. Imagine if we took someone to court every time they thought about something. Let's say that someone thought about doing a bank robbery and was taken to court for thinking it.

The prosecution stands and says, *"This person has been thinking about robbing a bank and is therefore a danger, a bad person, and should be imprisoned".* Then the defence comes and says, *"Well, there is not an actual crime; he has not, in fact, robbed a bank".* What would the jury say? They are most likely to say, *"Well, the person might think it, but we cannot convict if he has not done it".*

We cannot control the thoughts that appear in our minds; they can come from anywhere. I remember when I was a new mum, and my daughter had colic. She cried almost all night long. I used to drive her at 2 a.m. in the morning just so she could fall asleep, then as soon as I put her to bed, she would start crying again.

Some nights, we both started crying. I was exhausted and felt sorry for her. I remember thinking if I just throw her out of the window. Obviously, I never did that, but it seemed like an option on a night when I barely had any energy to hold her anymore. Perhaps some other mums can relate to this or similar thoughts?

The thoughts come and go; it is all about the meaning we put on them that matters. I could have beaten myself up forever thinking something so horrible, which meant I was a bad mum. But it was just a passing thought and did not carry any meaning or weight about who I was and my deep love for my daughter.

Tips for thoughts and beliefs

- When you notice yourself having any of the above types of thinking habits, Stop and take a step back. Notice the thought and make a note on a piece of paper or your phone. You can also use the **Daily Even Record Form** on the next page.
- Is this a fact or just an opinion? What is the evidence for and against this belief?
- Research suggests that flexible thinking correlates with healthy mental well-being, and rigid thinking correlates with mental health problems. Notice if there is any rigidity in your thinking, and watch out for "always, never" statements.
- Remember, you are the master of your mind, the CEO. Meditation and Mindfulness, which we look at in later chapters, will help you with this mastery.

You can download free ebooks, worksheets, audio guided meditation and attention training on https://www.mindandmood.co.uk/resources/

Situation (What happened)	My thoughts (Accusations)	Emotions (How I feel about the accusations)	Prosecution (Evidence to support accusations)	Defence Lawyer (Evidence against the accusations)	The Jury The rational outcome - A different perspective

Daily Event Record Form

Chapter 5

Decoding Perfectionist
Emotions and Behaviours

How is your perfectionist thinking affecting your emotions and behaviour?

The thoughts and beliefs that we have been exploring in the previous chapter, what do they do? What happens when we think of those thoughts? We have already looked at the CBT way of how a situation triggers unhelpful thoughts and limiting beliefs, affecting our physiology and behaviour. We can all agree on the negative impact of *"Perfectionism"* thinking on your emotions.

Let's take a deep dive into the emotional world of a perfectionist!

FEAR!

In my experience, fear is often the underlying emotion that drives many of the negative behaviours associated with perfectionism. Perfectionism can trigger an intense fear of failure, which can drive us to work harder, set impossibly high standards, and avoid taking risks or trying new things.

I would also like to add the fear of being judged or criticised by others, leading to seek constant validation and approval. Additionally, perfectionists may fear being *"found out"* as not being as competent or capable as others perceive them to be, which can lead to feelings of imposter syndrome and self-doubt.

All of these fears can be rooted in a deep sense of insecurity and a need to control one's environment to avoid experiencing perceived failure or inadequacy. Addressing these fears and developing healthy coping strategies can be an important step in managing perfectionism and improving overall well-being.

Let's look at some of the other main emotions experienced by perfectionists.

Stress

Stress is about the pressure that is happening here and now. It could be caused by an exam period, an important presentation or project, while juggling picking up children from school, etc. Perfectionists become stressed due to constantly striving for perfection or an ideal standard.

People who experience stress while trying to reach extremely high standards, often feel a sense of pressure to excel in all areas of their lives, including work, relationships, and personal goals. They may have difficulty accepting anything less than perfect and be overly self-critical or self-blaming when they fall short of their expectations.

Perfectionism stress can lead to a number of negative consequences, including anxiety, depression, burnout, and physical health problems. It can also interfere with relationships, as people may become so focused on their own performance that they neglect the needs and feelings of others.

If you put yourself under constant pressure of unrealistic expectations, prolonged stress can cause serious anxiety problems.

Anxiety

In the previous chapter, we discussed the difference between when we are in real danger and when we perceive that something bad might happen in the future. Every time we predict that something bad might happen, our brain perceives this as if it is currently happening because this part of the brain cannot distinguish the real or perceived threat, so we set off a chain reaction in our body to fight or flight (or freeze).

People with perfectionism anxiety often experience a pervasive sense of pressure to excel in all areas of their lives, including work, school, and personal goals. They set unrealistic expectations for themselves and are overly critical of their own performance, leading to self-doubt, insecurity, and fear of failure.

Perfectionism anxiety can be debilitating and interfere with daily functioning. It can lead to a range of negative consequences, including chronic anxiety, anxiety disorders, depression, and even physical health problems.

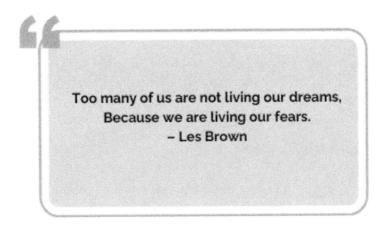

Too many of us are not living our dreams,
Because we are living our fears.
– Les Brown

Frustration

Frustration is a common experience for people who struggle with perfectionism. Perfectionists tend to set very high standards for themselves and may have difficulty accepting anything less than perfect. When you fall short of your high expectations, you may experience a range of negative emotions, including frustration, disappointment, annoyance and self-criticism. This applies to your expectations from others as well.

This can be particularly challenging because it can lead to a sense of stagnation or paralysis, as you may be reluctant to take risks or try new things for fear of failing to meet your own standards. This can prevent you from learning and growing, ultimately hindering your progress towards your goals.

Exhaustion

How often did you find yourself repeatedly going through the same report, email, or proposition before sending it? I used to find something to be changed/corrected each time I went through something. I would do it so many times that, in the end, I would lose sight of it and the feel for it. Working on a report until it is perfect, missing dinner and sleep, and ending up exhausted is just another normal day for a perfectionist.

Overwhelm

Trying to do everything to a degree so it is flawless takes a lot of time. I mean A LOT! So, you possibly end up spending double, triple the time on things than many other people would. As a result, things may start piling up at work and home and become overwhelming.

One of my clients, who was a mechanic for luxurious cars, found himself spending an extreme amount of time servicing each car. The company had set an average time for each car to be serviced, but he could only service one car a day because he checked the cars repeatedly until he was sure everything was perfect. This resulted in a queue of cars he needed to check, and the deadlines became shorter and shorter for the following cars, and he felt overwhelmed and guilty for rushing the others.

Shame

People who struggle with perfectionism often experience a sense of shame when they make mistakes or fail to achieve their goals, as they may view these experiences as evidence of their own inadequacy or failure. This can lead to a cycle of self-criticism and negative self-talk, which can further fuel feelings of shame and inadequacy.

Feeling shame can be difficult to acknowledge or talk about. If you struggle with perfectionism, you may feel ashamed of your perfectionistic tendencies, as you may perceive them as weaknesses or flaws.

Anger

Anger can also be a common emotion if you struggle with perfectionism, although it may not be the overarching emotion driving your behaviour. Perfectionists may become angry when they perceive that their high standards are not being met by themselves or others. They may also become frustrated or irritated when things do not go as planned or feel like they are not in control of a situation.

It is also common for a perfectionist to direct their anger inward, becoming self-critical and judgmental when they fail to meet their own high standards. This can lead to feelings of shame, guilt, and self-doubt.

It's important to note that anger, like all emotions, is a normal and healthy response to certain situations, but what you do with it is important. For example, Anger is just an emotion for us to deal with satiation when we are unfairly treated, but if we start hitting the walls, throwing things around, or interfering with daily functioning, it may be a sign of underlying issues that must be addressed.

Disappointment

Perfectionism often leads to a significant and recurring emotion: disappointment. When you set unrealistically high standards upon yourself and others, you can become deeply invested in achieving flawless outcomes. However, due to the inherent nature of perfectionism, it is nearly impossible to meet these unattainable expectations consistently. As a result, when perceived imperfections or failures occur, disappointment floods in.

The disappointment experienced by perfectionists is often intense and accompanied by feelings of frustration, self-criticism, and a sense of falling short. This emotion can be overwhelming and can fuel the cycle of perfectionism as individuals strive even harder to avoid future disappointment, perpetuating the cycle of unattainable standards.

Moreover, disappointment can become a persistent emotion due to the tendency to focus on the gap between reality and the idealised outcome. You might have a vivid image in your mind of how things should be, and when reality fails to align with that image, a deep sense of disappointment occurs. This emotion can undermine self-confidence, trigger self-doubt, and crumble self-esteem, as you might interpret your perceived shortcomings as personal failures. Over time, the repeated experience of disappointment can contribute to feelings of hopelessness and dissatisfaction, preserving the perfectionistic cycle and making it challenging to break free from its grip.

Sadness

Sadness is a common emotion experienced by perfectionists. If you are a perfectionist, you might often find yourself placing immense pressure on yourself to meet impossible standards, constantly striving for flawlessness. However, this relentless pursuit can lead to a perpetual state of dissatisfaction.

As a result, it is inevitable to frequently find yourself overwhelmed by a profound sense of sadness. This sadness stems from a deep awareness of your perceived shortcomings, a feeling of never being good enough, and a persistent longing for a level of achievement that feels forever out of reach.

Furthermore, perfectionism can breed sadness by fostering a constant fear of failure and a relentless *focus* on flaws and mistakes. Perfectionists are hypercritical of their performance and harshly judge themselves for any perceived misstep. This self-criticism, coupled with a tendency to compare oneself unfavourably to others, can contribute to feelings of sadness and despair, leading to a continuous cycle of disappointment and a lingering sense of sadness that can impact overall well-being and quality of life.

Demotivation

Perfectionists often experience a sense of demotivation due to their fear of failure or making mistakes. The overwhelming pressure to achieve flawless results can lead to feelings of paralysis or avoidance, as the fear of not meeting their own high standards becomes paralysing. Constantly pursuing perfection can drain their enthusiasm and make tasks feel overwhelming or unattainable.

Emotion regulation with the parasympathetic nervous system

In the brain chapter, we have talked about the sympathetic system being rapid and unconscious, an automatic reaction to protect the person from danger. The other system is the *"parasympathetic system"* that helps you calm yourself down. It is not automatic; you must consciously try to do so.

For example, work deadlines, worry, and fears can trigger this cascade of hormones for fight or flight that we have looked at. The parasympathetic nervous system acts as a brake, actively engaging. The more you practice, the better you become at relaxing your body.

How to engage the parasympathetic nervous system to calm ourselves down

- We always find peace in nature, so spend time in nature.
- Take time to do deep breathing (there are several breathing techniques, some of them are in this book as well).
- Meditate.
- Get regular massage.
- Well balanced nutrition.
- Find a soothing word, perhaps of a place where you feel calm and peaceful.
- Get enough sleep.
- Stroke animals.
- Practice yoga, chi kung, or tai chi.
- Do any of those *"Mindfully"*.

- Practice self-care and self-compassion (You can learn more about self-compassion and Mindfulness techniques in Chapter 9).

People often say, "It's so nice; we always escape to nature". Going out for walks, filling our lungs with fresh air, spending time in nature, and noticing the colours and sounds around us are great ways to nurture your parasympathetic nervous system to calm your mind and body.

The research suggests that doing the task in hand mindfully is more beneficial than doing a hobby with your mind elsewhere. For example, if you like gardening, do it mindfully. Do not allow your mind to go and worry about things when you're doing an enjoyable activity. Be there, be in the moment, and give yourself permission to enjoy that moment. Set a separate time for things that worry you and use the *"Worry crashing problem solver"* sheet under *"Perfectionism related behaviour"*. I will be talking about Mindfulness in more detail in Chapter 9.

Perfectionism related behaviour

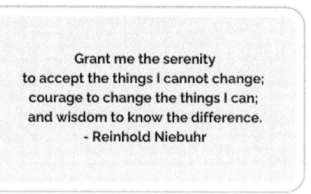

> Grant me the serenity
> to accept the things I cannot change;
> courage to change the things I can;
> and wisdom to know the difference.
> - Reinhold Niebuhr

There are many things we do or don't do in order to avoid the uncomfortable feeling caused by perfectionist thinking. I will cover the most common ones, some of which you might recognise.

Worry

Does your perfectionism cause you much worry? Do you believe worrying helps you prepare for the worst?

Many people say they feel worried; however, worry is not a feeling but a behaviour that becomes a habit over time. It has much to do with the desire to know what might happen in the future as a consequence of a decision you have made or a step you have taken and the intolerance of uncertainty.

"What if it is not the right decision that will give the perfect result?"
"What if it is a mistake?"

Then comes the *"Catastrophising,"* followed by overestimating the possibility of something bad happening and underestimating your own ability to cope. Sometimes, my clients say to me, "Oh, you know, I'm a worrier, I have always been a worrier".

Do you remember we talked about what you practice grows stronger? If you worry a lot, you get really good at worrying. And that is what makes us worriers. There are, of course, genetic dispositions that are worth mentioning; however, the principle of the pathways in the brain that create habits still prevails.

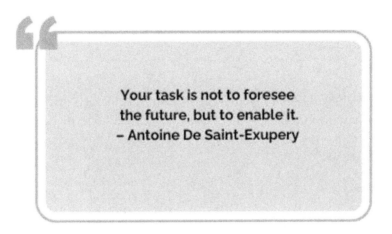

Your task is not to foresee the future, but to enable it. – Antoine De Saint-Exupery

Sometimes, we have some positive beliefs about worry, which keep the worrying behaviour going. Some believe it will help them prepare their work better or make better decisions, explore all possibilities you believe might help you prepare, or simply prepare if and when the worst happens.

Let's have a look at what is helpful to worry about and what is not. I guess we can categorise these as hypothetical worries and helpful worries. The first thing is to notice that you are actually worrying. If you find many "what if"s going around in your mind, you are most likely worrying.

Hypothetical Worry	Helpful Worry
• Notice what you are worried about. • Is there a solution if you think about it for hours? • If the answer is no, make a conscious decision to let go. • It will only burn up your brainpower. • Steal your precious time and cause anxiety. • Move your attention (spotlight) to something more meaningful.	• Notice what you are worried about. • Is there anything I can do about this? Now or later? • If later, schedule. • Write down possible solutions. • Look at the pros and cons of each possible solution. • Pick one that sounds the best. • Take action. • Review - If not ideal, choose the next possible solution.

The most important question to ask yourself when you notice the worry is:

"Is there anything I can do about this now or later?"

If the answer is a straight **"no"**, it means even if you give yourself 24 or 48 hours or how many hours you want to worry, you will still not find an answer or a solution. It is a false sense of "problem-solving" for a problem that does not exist. Worrying about solving a problem that does not exist will burn your brainpower and take away from the enjoyment of your present moment.

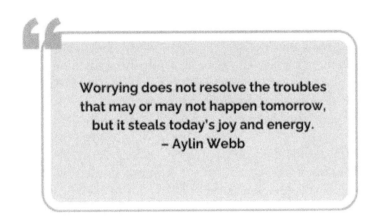

Worrying does not resolve the troubles
that may or may not happen tomorrow,
but it steals today's joy and energy.
– Aylin Webb

A hypothetical worry can be, for example;

"What if someone hits my car while it is parked in front of my house?"
"What if my cat gets in a fight and dies while outside?"

You might be worrying about it for days, feeling anxious, and watching & checking up on your car all the time, but no amount of worry is going to change anything. You are guessing, and your mind is racing to find hundreds of possibilities for this to happen and try to find solutions to all of those possibilities.

In reality, only - if at all, one of those possibilities can happen in a certain situation. Worrying will steal your precious time and cause you a lot of anxiety. Move your focus to something that will add value to your life and your mood.

It is easier said than done, but it is certainly possible by training your mind. Mindfulness practices and meditation help teach our minds to focus on what we want on the spotlight and not let our minds wander and decide what the spotlight shall be.

The helpful worry, on the other hand, can help us resolve an existing problem or a problem lying ahead. When you notice it, just ask yourself the same question again;

"Is there anything I can do about this now or later?"

If you do not need to do it now, schedule it to attend to it later and move on with your day.

If the answer is "yes and now", then work on the ways that can help you solve the problem. Have a look at the "Worry-crashing problem solver" sheet on the next page.

First, write down the problem and 3-4 possible solutions. Doing nothing can also count as one of the solutions. Take 2 of the solutions and look at the pros and cons of each solution. Pick one that seems the best out of the two, take action, give it a chance, and review.

Worry-crashing problem solver

Step 1: The problem I worry about is:

Step 2: The possible solutions are (Anything you can think of):
1.
2.
3.
4.
5.
Step 3: Choose the two that look better than the others:

Step 4: Pros and cons of the two you have chosen.

Pros	Cons
1	1
2	2

Step 5: Pick the one that looks like the better solution:

Step 6: Action steps and timings:

Step 7: Review:

Step 8: Any changes to be made, or if the first one did not work, pick the other one and repeat the process.

Procrastination

In the paper titled "The Nature of Procrastination" published in 2007 by Piers Steel, it was reported that approximately 80-95% of college students engaged in procrastination, around 15-20% of adults reported that they procrastinate consistently, and approximately 40% of people have experienced financial loss due to procrastination.

These numbers highlight that procrastination is a fairly common issue, with a substantial percentage of various populations reporting experiences with procrastination to differing degrees. It is a pervasive phenomenon and has been linked to a variety of negative outcomes, including decreased mental health and well-being.

So, what really is procrastination?

Procrastination is delaying and putting off tasks until the last minute, even though you know it has negative consequences, acting against your better judgement, knowing that it is not good for you. You are completely aware of the fact that you should be doing your tasks, and you probably have it at the back of your head, luring you all the time, but you still don't do the task and do everything else instead.

When I was studying and needed to do my assignments, I used to find myself doing the washing, the cleaning and so on. I knew I had something more important to do, but I still did everything else. You do easier activities and avoid the uncomfortable feeling because when you sit down to do this task, it feels uncomfortable. What is behind that?

It can cause anxiety, panic, depression, and physical health problems due to exhaustion and stress. Professor Grantham suggests that procrastination is mostly about emotions and avoiding discomfort. We look for easier tasks with rewards instead of sitting down and doing the task that feels uncomfortable. Our brain likes rewards because we release dopamine, which is the "feel good" hormone. So, we will keep going for the rewarding tasks, avoiding the uncomfortable.

And so it can become addictive because of that. And when you don't do it, there is no risk, you know, you don't risk anything bad. And that's the short-term gain. It's good in the short term and relieves you but it becomes problematic in the long term. Some beliefs keep it going, thinking well, it won't take much time, and I'm better motivated at the last moment. I work better under pressure, so those beliefs would keep it going.

The issue about procrastination is not about time management, because research found that time management techniques actually do not help procrastination. When you are procrastinating, there is also that pressure from others. If you are at work, the work piles up, and you might find yourself just doing other things, feeling guilty about putting off the task.

So why do we procrastinate, then? Does it have to do with fear of failure? When we know it's not good for us and makes us feel guilty, as the deadline comes closer, we get stressed, anxious, and not to mention the feeling of guilt soaring.

For perfectionists, the fear of not getting it perfect is usually at the essence of procrastination. So, what happens when we procrastinate:

- Delaying or putting off tasks until the last minute despite the negative consequences.
- Acting against your better judgement. You know it is good for you to do it, but you still don't.
- Doing everything else less important first than the task at hand.
- Easier activities that override bad, uncomfortable feelings.
- Not about time management or laziness.
- Procrastinators are not chilled; in fact, they are quite stressed about the work they have not done yet.
- Pressure from others and the feeling of guilt for putting off the task.
- Can cause anxiety, panic, depression and physical health issues.
- It is about emotions.
- We always look for rewards, avoiding the uncomfortable feeling - Addictive habit.
- There is no risk, safe, short-term gain - problematic long-term.
- It won't take much time - I am better-motivated last moment.

The Eisenhower Matrix Planning Guide might be helpful for those who tend to procrastinate. Look at what is urgent and needs our attention, and we have to set time for it in small goal settings. And then there are the not urgent things we would like to schedule to do later.

If others can do any of the tasks you need, delegate it. Then there are things that are not important. As a perfectionist, you may think that others may not do it as good as you; however, make a conscious effort to delegate. Ensure you eliminate all distractions, so you can focus on the task.

IMPORTANT & URGENT

Do it now!

Things with clear deadlines and consequences.

Examples:
Paying urgent bills
Finishing a project with a close deadline
Preparing for a client meeting

IMPORTANT & NOT URGENT

Schedule it

Important but not very urgent tasks.

Examples:
Planning exercise days
Networking event
Professional development

NOT IMPORTANT & URGENT

Delegate it

Things that need to be done, but can also be done by others.

Examples:
Responding to some of the emails
Admin work
Laying the dinner table

NOT IMPORTANT & NOT URGENT

Delete it

Distractions that hold you back and can make you feel bad afterwords. Ok in moderation.

Examples:
Social media scrolling
Video games
Watching TV

The Eisenhower Matrix Planning Guide.

Top tips for procrastination

- Taking action – using SMART Goals - Specific, Measurable, Achievable, Realistic and Time-based.
- Clarify what tasks are urgent, what tasks are priority and what can wait.
- Break down into smaller tasks. List every step and possible problems and resources. Task list of focus for each day.
- Visualise how it will look when you complete it.
- What is your motivation for doing the task?
- Notice your avoidance. Is it too complex and overwhelming? Freeze?
- You have too many tasks and need to look at "urgencies and priorities" (Eisenhower matrix).
- Be aware of your focus span and take breaks every 20-30 minutes.
- Set your intention each day: What do you want to achieve by the end of the day?
- Observe your thoughts and feelings when you tend to procrastinate.

Avoidance

The perfectionist sometimes chooses to avoid rather than fail. A typical example would be learning a new language but not speaking it because you have not mastered it perfectly. You might also end up giving up learning new things, i.e., playing an instrument, because you are not doing it perfectly.

Avoiding situations that may be challenging for your perfectionist thinking is also a common behaviour. You may fear that you will not be the perfect entertainer or have the perfect dress on, and people will find you boring and choose not to attend social gatherings.

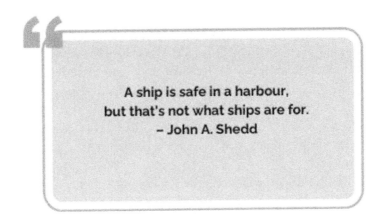

A ship is safe in a harbour,
but that's not what ships are for.
– John A. Shedd

This will reduce your anxiety in the short run, but it will cause loneliness due to lack of connection with others, guilt, shame and depression in the long run. Some other examples could be not sending job applications with the fear that you may not get the job, not asking for a pay rise because you might get rejection, not having a relationship because the person may not live up to your expectations or abandon you.

Top avoidance tips:

- Find why you would like to learn what you are learning.
- What are the pros and cons of doing it and not doing it
- Challenge the thought: what is the evidence to prove this? Do you have any evidence against it?

Decision making

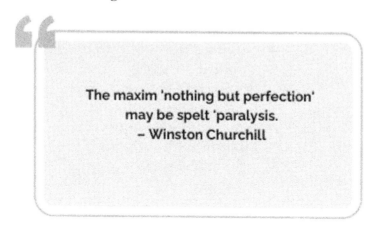

> **The maxim 'nothing but perfection' may be spelt 'paralysis.**
> **– Winston Churchill**

I have put decision-making here because even though it is a cognitive process, for perfectionists, the amount of analysis to find the perfect decision could be quite numbing, and we end up doing nothing. The paralysis of analysis!

Many of us might be analysing the situations before making decisions, but how long is a reasonable amount of time before making a decision? Sometimes, the decision-making process, analysing all possible outcomes and trying to find the *"perfect"* decision to achieve the perfect outcome can really cause paralysis.

You may want to write a proposal, even an email, or decide what to cook for dinner guests, but you simply cannot decide or take a really long time because it has to be perfect.
What to wear, what colour of the dress to buy, can't decide the best restaurant until it is too late.

There are several things that drive this, i.e., fear of failure & judgement, comparison and anxiety caused by the fear of a less favourable outcome.

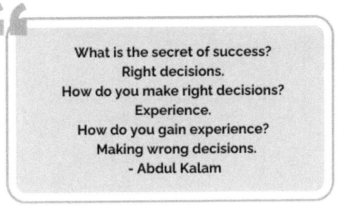

What is the secret of success?
Right decisions.
How do you make right decisions?
Experience.
How do you gain experience?
Making wrong decisions.
- Abdul Kalam

Checking and re-checking – Causing slowness

Research shows that perfectionist standards are associated with reduced efficiency (Eysneck & Stoeber, 2008). The perfectionists' unrealistically high standards also emerge on checking behaviour, often to ensure there is no mistake, the task is completed perfectly, immaculate, flawless, clean and so on.

Several reasons cause the checking behaviour:

Fear of embarrassment.
Fear of being judged by others.
Fear of failure.
Fearing the worst-case scenario, if you make a mistake.
Inflated responsibility for others.
Fear of criticism.

Any other reasons? Write down what your reasons are for excessive checking.

_____
_____
_____
_____

Here are a few facts:

- Repeated checking does not prevent mistakes.
- Decreases confidence in your memory and abilities.
- Increases uncertainty and anxiety (Shafran, 2010).

You keep checking things, perhaps because you don't want to make a mistake due to the fear of embarrassment. The assumption is it will be embarrassing if I make a mistake. You might be checking the clock so as not to be late for a meeting, checking documents and emails, and not to have any spelling mistakes. There is the assumption of others' expectations of you and that they will always judge harshly. Research shows that perfectionist standards are associated with reduced efficiency. Checking over and over again does not prevent mistakes. It decreases confidence in your memory and abilities because you check so much that you lose sight and, in the end, you are not quite sure.

Did I check it? Did I check page two? Did I check the door? I'm not so sure. Should I check it again? It causes increased uncertainty and, as a result, anxiety. As you can see, we are back to anxiety again—the constant perceived threat to the system causing stress due to relentless standards and putting high pressure upon ourselves.

There is a certain peak where we perform at our best. We need to be motivated, and that is where we perform our best. If we keep repeating our work over, we are using too much energy on the same task. And we can end up getting burnout, decreased concentration, focus, and we're more likely to make mistakes because we will be exhausted. It might be easier to see it on the "Yerkes & Dodson Law" Table.

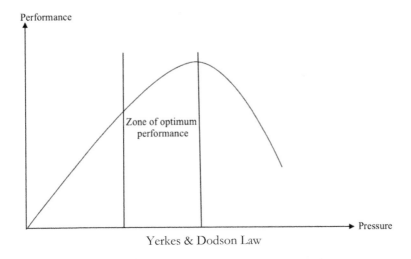

Yerkes & Dodson Law

Ishida (2005) and Stoeber and Eysenck (2008) also found in their research that high levels of perfectionism were associated with lower efficiency.

Constantly checking work to make sure there are no mistakes.
Frequently checking time.
Re-checking emails written to others over and over again before sending.
Reading news slowly to make sure you don't miss a thing.

Top tips for checking

- Question and challenge the fear.
- What is the worst thing that can happen, and what are your resources to cope (Internal and external).
- Change the narrative in your head to a positive mindset.
- Remember the number of times that it went well.
- Think of the times you made mistakes; did they pass?
- Decide to check x amount of times and stay with it
- Move your attention elsewhere.

- Think of more meaningful things you can do with your precious time.
- Will it matter in 5 years?
- Apply the anxiety-reducing tips from this session, which we will look at shortly.
- If someone you care about made a mistake, would you judge them harshly? If not, why the double standards? Be kind to yourself.

Some more of the other perfectionist behaviours are below:

Reassurance seeking

This usually results from losing confidence in yourself and your abilities due to over checking, worrying, procrastinating and not trusting your abilities to make the right decisions. Some examples are checking with others that results are acceptable and the need for compliments (for work, cooked meals, etc.).

Excessive organising, list-making

Excessive organising and list-making are common traits among perfectionists, driven by the desire for control and order. It may provide a sense of temporary relief or reassurance, but it can also become overwhelming and time-consuming. While organising and making lists can be helpful for productivity and planning, it's important to strike a balance and avoid becoming too rigid or fixated on perfection in these activities.

Trying to change other people

For perfectionists, trying to change other people can be a common inclination driven by the desire for everything to meet their high standards. They may feel frustrated or dissatisfied when others don't live up to their expectations. Some examples are correcting others about how things should be done and inflexibility about how others should be and should do things.

Overcompensating

Overcompensating is common among perfectionists, stemming from their fear of failure or not being good enough. They may go to extreme lengths to prove their worth, often taking on excessive responsibilities or striving for unattainable levels of achievement. However, overcompensating can lead to burnout, stress, and a constant feeling of never being satisfied. Arriving 30 minutes before the appointment time, taking on too much work, and always saying yes to friends are some examples of overcompensating.

Correcting

Perfectionists can have a strong desire for precision and accuracy, constantly needing to fix and perfect things. You might find, for example, that the laundry must be folded perfectly so all the edges match; if it is not perfect, it does not deserve to be in the cupboard.

Failure to delegate

Failure to delegate is a common struggle for perfectionists, driven by the belief that they are the only ones who can complete a task to their high standards. They often have a strong desire for control and fear that delegating tasks will lead to mistakes. However, this mindset can lead to overwhelm, burnout, and a lack of efficiency.

You might find yourself believing that you have to do everything yourself because you don't trust that others can do it to high standards. Or perhaps not having a cleaner, because they cannot do it as properly as you.

Top tips

- Square breathing exercise – Breath in down to your diaphragm while counting to 4, hold your breath for 4 counts, breathe out for 4 counts and hold again for 4 counts. This would make a square. Repeat this daily and, when needed, at least 3-4 times.
- Stop and slow right down, practically everything, for a moment, and the world will still keep turning. Just repeat the word "slow down" to yourself regularly.
- Stop and observe your thoughts and emotions like a fly on the wall. Watch what is happening in the room.
- Move the focus of your attention to elsewhere, just like on a stage. The spotlight shines on what you focus on— practice moving it to different areas of your own will .
- Listen to music that you enjoy. A 2013 research "The Effect of Music on the Human Stress Response Myriam V. Thoma and collegues found that music had a positive effect on participants' mood, helping to reduce stress and improve emotional regulation.
- Self-acceptance is a part of our growth, and a rigid outlook on ourselves always correlates with high levels of stress. Blaming a decision made with what we know now, which we did not know in the past, is simply being unfair on ourselves.
- You are enough.
- Your journey is unique.
- Remind yourself that *"self-worth"* is not dependent on *"success"*.
- What you may call a *"failure"* is actually a *"bounce"*, which is necessary for personal growth and development.
- Question and challenge the fear.
- What is the worst thing that can happen, and what are your resources to cope (Internal and external)?
- Change the narrative in your head to a positive mindset. Remember the amount of times that it went well.

- Think of the times you made mistakes; did they pass? Decide to check x amount of times and stick with it.
- Think of more meaningful things you can do with your precious time.
- Will it matter in 5 years?

Weekly goals suggestions:
Set 1 intention each day this week.
Work on changing 1 limiting belief about yourself this week and look for evidence - opening up the RAS (Reticular Activating System).
Pick up one hobby that you used to enjoy or have been wanting to try for a long time.

You can download free ebooks, worksheets, audio guided meditation and attention training on https://www.mindandmood.co.uk/resources/

Chapter 6

Self-Esteem: Unlocking Inner Worth

Self-esteem issues are tightly connected to perfectionism and for really good reasons. For perfectionists, self-worth is based on outperforming others, personal competence and the approval of others.

> **You build confidence within yourself**
> **by trusting in who you are,**
> **and what you stand for.**
> **– Aylin Webb**

Imagine that nothing is ever good enough unless it is spotless and that the only feedback you will accept is the positive one; no mistake, no weakness, no shortcoming is ever allowed, and if any of the above happens, it is a disaster, and you are absolutely useless, a failure, never good enough. Not only that, but others always do better.

Self-esteem is about a sense of self-worth, self-value, and just accepting and respecting yourself with all your strengths, shortcomings and abilities to cope when things go wrong.

One of the issues that keeps coming up with low self-esteem is when we keep saying yes to everything because we fear that they may not like us when we say no. We fear rejection and ultimately being left out and lonely. This lies very innate inside of us, from the times of tribes, where our survival was dependent on being a part of the tribe.

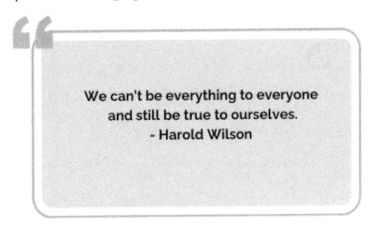

> **We can't be everything to everyone and still be true to ourselves.**
> **- Harold Wilson**

Sometimes we don't communicate our wants and needs with fear of being rejected. If there are more people who might disagree, you may just go with the flow if you have low self-esteem.

You can see how constantly trying to do everything absolutely perfectly can lead to low self-esteem because we are not superhumans, and perfect does not exist. Let's do a little exercise and see who you think is the most perfect person/flawless and the one as far from being any good at all/full of flaws.

If you think of a continuum, who would be the most perfect person, rating 10, and who would be the most imperfect person for you, rating 0? Put some names on each end; it could be celebrities, well-known people or some people in your life.

Now start filling in the other numbers with other people, a little less perfect at 9 – 8, etc. Where do you fit in? What number are you?

0--10
Most imperfect   Most perfect

Now, think about why you think of these numbers for these people. The person at 10, are they really absolutely flawless? Is that really possible?

What is self-esteem?

Self-esteem is a deep recognition of our self-worth, acting as an internal compass that defines our self-value and self-respect. It goes beyond confidence in our abilities. It's about embracing our strengths and accepting our flaws. It gives us a strong sense of belonging empowering us to feel competent and capable when facing challenges.

Rooted in our identity self-esteem helps us recognise our rights from wrongs and stay aligned with our deeply held values. I also think that healthy self-esteem equips us with the bravery to stand our ground even if it means disagreeing with the majority and to communicate our opinions without fear of rejection. A well-developed sense of self-worth empowers us to assertively say 'no' when something is not ok. We will explore "assertion" deeper in Chapter 7.

My client Dorothy had a difficult childhood. Her parents were too busy with their work, otherwise arguing and not paying attention to their children. She had two older brothers; most of the time, they teased her and made fun of her. She always felt alone at home and was quite an introvert. Dorothy was lonely as a child and believed no one liked her. She thought other kids must be better than her because they all hang out together and have fun. She felt that she was an outcast and that something must be wrong with her.

Dorothy did well in school, getting high grades, and realised that this was the only time she got other people's positive attention, including her parents. Her teachers were praising her, and it felt really good. Dorothy kept studying harder, spending days and nights on her projects and exams, and if any of her friends asked her to join them, she always preferred to stay in and study, not face the risk of being judged by others.

Dorothy's world fell apart if she scored anything less than A or A*. She got angry with herself, put herself down, called herself stupid, and did not want to speak with anyone. She did not get the first job she applied for, and she took that again as a personal rejection and decided she was simply a failure.

Dorothy had achieved high standards academically and was now holding a high management position in a corporate firm. When she came to me for coaching, she had high levels of stress and anxiety, because she was worried that she would make a mistake and lose her job that she wanted for so many years.

During our sessions, we have explored Dorothy's automatic thoughts, assumptions and where her unhelpful beliefs came from. We also made a formulation in order to understand what kept the maintenance cycle. This way, Dorothy could decide how she could break the cycle, pull out her strengths and emphasise her positive qualities, start taking time for her self-care, and her self-esteem started building up. Not only had Dorothy discovered her self-worth and built up her confidence to live a joyful life, she also started recognising when others were in similar situations and recommended them to come and see me, which I took as a compliment.

Let's have a look at low self-esteem the CBT way:

Type of thoughts
We constantly think that others are better than we are, negatively impacting our self-confidence.
Critical self (recognise that from Perfectionism?).
Doubting yourself.
Dismissing successes and strengths.
Unable to accept praise and compliments.
Blaming yourself for everything that goes wrong.
Blowing mistakes out of proportion.
Focusing on perceived weaknesses, shortcomings (also physically) and self-criticism.
Worrying about rejection (worry is a behaviour but with future related thoughts).
Low opinion about self and self-worth.
Thinking you are less than others.
Never enough.

Emotions
Anxiety
Guilt
Anger
Sadness
Snappiness
Frustration
Shame
Extremely upset with criticism or disapproval
Low mood
Hopelessness

Type of behaviour
Not trusting yourself enough to make decisions - it may not be the perfect decision.
Avoiding challenges and opportunities with fear of losing face, failing, making mistakes or not doing it perfectly.
Always putting yourself and self-care last - perception of others' expectations and trying to please others all the time.
Avoidance of social situations - worrying about not being the perfect entertainer, perfectly dressed, perfectly looking, etc., and people may judge.
Hesitant, avoiding eye contact.
Apologising.
Not able to accept compliments.
Unable to assert yourself and draw clear lines.
Unable to say no to extra workload.

Bodily sensations
Muscle tension
Insomnia
Exhaustion
Symptoms of anxiety and depression
Fatigue
Tension
Low energy

A heightened sense of awareness of self, specifically about what others may think of you, about how you look, behave, etc.

Low self-esteem can have an impact on different areas of life:

Work: Underperforming – avoid challenges and opportunities – push themselves very hard to cover up their inabilities or lack of skills.

Relationships: Self-consciousness, oversensitive to criticism or disapproval (self-worth based on outside resources), excessive eagerness to please others, withdrawal from intimacy.

Some adopt a policy of being the life and soul of the party, appearing confident and in control, and always putting others first; otherwise, they believe people won't want them.

Leisure: Avoiding activities with the risk of being judged, i.e., art or dance classes, and not relaxing to enjoy self.

Self-care: Not taking proper care of oneself, missing dentist appointments because of work, drinking excessively, and smoking.

You will find Melanie Fennel's (1997) CBT formulation for self-esteem on the next page. See if you can fill it in with your own relative issues and think about how you can break the cycle.

CBT MODEL OF LOW SELF ESTEEM

Early experiences

Important life events, difficult past experiences

Core/limiting beliefs

Overly negative limited beliefs, negative biases

Rules for Living assumptions.

(if... then... /Shoulds and musts)

Triggering situation

Activation of belief

Depression symptoms

Predictions

Anxiety Symptoms

Self critical thinking

Unhelpful behaviours

Confirmation of the
Limiting belief

Melanie Fennell's formulation of self-esteem (1997)

I think quite an important one about self-esteem is thinking that you're less than others, that others are better than you are. And then, of course, there's that worry about rejection, that I will be rejected. That really is the one that causes a lot of issues with being unable to say no, even if it is a big price to pay. You can see how perfectionism and low self-esteem are often tightly knitted together. It's healthy to want to be able to face challenges, grow, and strive; but it's equally important to accept your mistakes, learn from them, and move on.

There are also physical perceptions about your body. Are my toes okay and nice looking or are my legs a bit too big or too thin or too thick or too long or too short. Is my weight, okay? There is a lot of self-consciousness about physical appearance and shortcomings of one's abilities, especially amongst women.

Remember, RAS, the Reticular Activating System; if you focus on those things as shortcomings, you will always filter and perceive them negatively. Whatever you focus on, RAS will bring you evidence. Out of millions of information out there, it will be screening in the information that will prove you right.

People with low self-esteem often put themselves last on the priority list with the fear of rejection and not feeling worthy of self-love and care. They just keep fulfilling other people's need. Of course, when we have these negative beliefs about ourselves, and when we are so self-conscious, even the thought of saying "no" causes negative emotions, such as anxiety, guilt and shame.

There is also anger, for example, if people keep asking you to do things for them. You get angry with yourself for having to do what they ask, and angry with them for asking. Sadness and snappiness come just a tad before anger, frustration and shame when your energy levels are low for trying to do everything perfectly. Of course, there is also fear of looking weak and vulnerable.

There will be muscle tension; you will have problems sleeping; you will feel tired and exhausted, as well as the symptoms of anxiety and depression. We have discussed those in our earlier chapters: heart racing, hands shaking, the adrenaline rush, the feeling in your stomach. Mind and body are connected, so you will feel these physical sensations in triggering situations.

What do you do? You have to deal with this and cope with it somehow. One of the unhelpful coping mechanisms is not trusting yourself enough to make decisions, because it may not be the perfect decision for the perfect outcome. If I make a decision here, it may go wrong, and people may blame me. You then shy away from making decisions to avoid challenges and opportunities that may be right in front of you because you are staying in your comfort zone.

I remember reading somewhere that *"if you don't look after yourself, then others don't get the best of you; they just get the rest of you"*. Trying to be the perfect someone for everyone and doing everything perfectly is not humanly possible, so look after yourself first so your loved ones can get the best of you and not the rest of you.

You can see how perfectionism and low self-esteem are often tightly knitted together. It's healthy to want to be able to face challenges, grow, and strive; but it's equally important to accept your mistakes, learn from them, and move on.

The perfectionist mindset is rigid, and there is no flexibility. The research shows that a rigid mindset about "shoulds and musts" correlates with mental health problems, and a flexible mindset about "coulds and woulds" correlates with joy, contentment and thrive.

Have a look at your rules and assumptions, gain awareness and review why you think that way. Where does it come from? We are born pure. Think where and when or how you have learned that you are not good enough. If you can't quite point it out, it is okay too. We don't dwell on the past; we just make sense of the present issues and work on changing towards more helpful ways.

What matters is how you think and how you feel now. Just review that. What's the evidence for your beliefs to be completely true? Is that a fact, or is it just an opinion, a feeling you have about yourself? Challenge them, check the evidence for and the evidence against them.

Are there people that you are worthy of their love and friendship? Think about all the positive qualities that people like about you and what you like about yourself. Make a conscious decision to replace the unhelpful beliefs with positive qualities and a positive mindset, then look for evidence to confirm those. Practice it daily, and you will start noticing the evidence filtering through that will prove you that your new belief is actually true. Your RAS (Reticular Activating System) will start working for your new beliefs.

Note down your personal positive qualities. Think about what kinds of positive values you have about yourself. Why do people like you? Why do your friends and family keep you around? Why do people call you? They ask how are you doing? They come when you need them. Regularly remember your achievements and people who love you.

It doesn't matter how small you think your achievements may be, just remember how much work you put into it to get there. Be mindful that perfectionists are good at underestimating their achievements. Nothing is too small, and it does not have to be work or academic achievement at all. **Selfish or selfless?** Imagine that you are a glass, and the water is your resources. You are constantly taking care of other people and using the resources in the glass. You are selfless because you put others before you, using all your resources.

Once you have used all the resources in the glass, you are trying to run on empty; there is nothing left for you, not for others, even though you are still trying to give to others and help others and do everything for them.

You're no good to yourself, and you're no good to others, either. If you actually fill yourself up with things that matter to you, look after yourself, do your recreation, fitness, health, whatever makes you happy, whatever is good for you. Take a hot shower or bath with candles, whatever makes you happy. Or be with your friends.

If you fill up this glass, it will be so full of you. So full of looking after you that this will be overflowing. And that overflow is enough for you and lots for the others around. This was something I saw on an Oprah Winfrey interview at Stanford University, which I thought was absolutely amazing. Oprah was talking about the difference between selfishness and selflessness. She said, *"I'm so full of myself, I'm so full of myself, I look after myself, and there's so much of it, it is overflowing and enough for everybody else around me as well"*.

A daily positive/gratitude diary really makes a difference. You might think, I don't have time for that. It will take you five minutes just to write down three things daily. You can go back to it months later and remember your blessings. It does make a difference when in doubt.

Schedule time for yourself and communicate your wants and needs. Remember, everybody has their own story. Slowly let go of comparing yourself with others.

How can I build self-esteem?

- Note down your positive personal qualities.
- Regularly remember your achievements, however small you may think they are. Remember how much work it took to get there.
- Do a daily positive diary/gratitude list, so you do not forget the good things.
- Record your inner critical voice and look for evidence for the opposite! Use the formulation RCRP=T on Chapter 2, page 34.
- Test out your assumptions.
- Are they your thoughts or the thoughts of others? How do you know? Fact or opinion?
- Make time for yourself – your self-care.
- Communicate your wants and needs assertively - it is ok to say "no".
- Do not compare yourself and your life with others; everyone has a story.
- Watch your inner critique and your communication with yourself.
- Change the *shoulds and musts* to *could and would like to.*
- Remember you are human, and every human on earth has got shortcomings and strengths.

You can download free ebooks, worksheets, audio guided meditation and attention training on https://www.mindandmood.co.uk/resources/

Chapter 7

Unlocking Confidence and Taking Charge with Assertion

Confidence

A lot of my clients come to me saying, *"I really lost my confidence; I want to be more confident about myself".* I think sometimes people confuse the two, but confidence and self-esteem are two different things.

People often talk about confidence as if it's a magical quality that some people are born with and others are not. But the truth is that confidence can be learned and developed over time. It's not something you are born with and never lose; in fact, everyone experiences moments of self-doubt and insecurity at some point.

Confidence is not a personality or a characteristic about you; it is a state and situational. Confidence is all about believing and relying on yourself to face challenges and just how well you can present your abilities and positive qualities in certain situations. It is not a way of being but changes from situation to situation.

We are not always confident or never confident. You can have confidence in yourself in some areas; well, I can do this; I'm really confident about this. And in some areas, you're not so confident because perhaps you lack knowledge, competence and experience. It's not necessarily something you're born with, or you are not born with it; *you can learn it, and you can build it.*

What is self-confidence?

So, what is confidence? In essence, confidence is a feeling of self-assurance and assurance in one's abilities. Confidence empowers individuals to take on challenges, pursue their goals, and navigate life's ups and downs with resilience.

It's the belief that you can handle whatever comes your way and have what it takes to be successful. When you're confident, you feel good about yourself and your capabilities – that feeling radiates outwards, influencing how you interact with others and the world around you.

Confidence is built upon a foundation of self-acceptance and self-belief. It arises from acknowledging one's strengths, talents, and accomplishments while accepting and learning from failures and setbacks. Cultivating confidence involves developing a positive and realistic self-image, recognising personal worth beyond external validation, and embracing a growth mindset that views challenges as opportunities for growth and learning.

It is important to note that confidence is not the same thing as arrogance or believing you can do no wrong. Arrogance is believing that you're better than everyone else. Confidence is about knowing your strengths and weaknesses. Just remember that confidence is not a static quality; it can be strengthened and made more resilient with practice.

Building confidence

Let's think of a situation; perhaps you are about to present to a big audience and feel anxious. You might worry by thinking that you might go blank, forget your words, make a fool of yourself and be embarrassed during the presentation. So you are not feeling confident and afraid that people will judge you; it will be awful.

Just listen to your inner voice and ask yourself what is happening here. Is it actually jeopardising what you are about to do and causing you anxiety? Then, think of the times you have done well. Tell yourself, *"I can do this, I feel confident, I'm capable"*. That is a great way to trick your mind. Once you change the narrative to positive inside your head, you will start feeling the effects of anxiety-reducing.

Think about all the times you have done similar things and finished with your head high. Think about all your abilities and qualities that will allow you to do this, and watch your posture of confidence.

The posture is really important. Imagine how a confident and competent person would look and visualise yourself the same way. Straight chest, shoulders slightly up and back, chin up rather than down, standing straight. It's okay to keep pretending to be confident and send your brain the message. Your brain will perceive, *"It will go okay; we are confident about this"*.

It is about how we talk, how we walk, how we move, how we think, our beliefs will affect how we feel. Think about Buddhism; it is all about the mindset. Think of your strengths and what will help you with this presentation and remind yourself of your achievements. And trust yourself in your abilities.

You can do many things to boost your confidence, both in the short and long term. Some of these include practising self-compassion, setting realistic goals, focusing on your strengths, accepting compliments, and surrounding yourself with positive people and people who love you for who you are.

The most important thing is to keep working on it, even if you don't see results right away. Confidence is something that can be built up over time, so don't get discouraged if it feels like you're struggling. Just keep working at it, and you'll eventually see progress.

So, is it possible to lose confidence? Yes, it is. But it's also possible to restore and rebuild it. The most important thing is to be mindful of your thoughts and behaviours and to make a conscious effort to boost your confidence when it starts to waver. With time and practice, you can develop a strong sense of self-assurance to help you navigate life's challenges.

And finally, can you always be confident? No, but that doesn't mean you can't get there. Building up your confidence takes time and effort, but it's definitely worth the effort in the end. Remember, confidence is something that can improve your life in a variety of ways, so don't give up on it. Just keep working at it, and you'll eventually see results.

Self-confidence is key to happiness and success. When you feel good about yourself, you can take on the world. However, if you are lacking in self-confidence, it can be difficult to achieve your goals. Here are a few steps you can take to get back your self-confidence and improve the way you feel about yourself.

1. Get organised: Feeling like you are in control of your life can boost your confidence levels. Start by creating a daily to-do list and sticking to it. Having a plan will make you feel more in control and help you feel better about yourself overall.

2. Dress for success: One of the easiest ways to feel better about yourself is to dress in a way that makes you feel confident. Wear clothes that make you feel like your best self, and don't be afraid to experiment until you find what works for you.

3. Set realistic goals: Don't set yourself up for failure by trying to accomplish things you know you can't. Instead, set realistic goals that you know you can achieve with little effort. When you accomplish something, even if it's small, it will make you feel good about yourself and boost your confidence.

4. Take care of yourself: It's important to take care of yourself both physically and mentally. Ensure you get enough sleep, eat healthy foods, and exercise regularly. Taking care of yourself will help you feel better about yourself and improve your confidence levels.

5. Accept compliments: When someone compliments you, don't brush it off. Accept the compliment and say thank you. Recognising and accepting your accomplishments will help you feel good about yourself and boost your confidence levels.

6. Surround yourself with positive people: Surrounding yourself with positive people can help boost your confidence levels. Negative people can bring you down, so make sure to spend time with people who make you feel good about yourself.

7. Let go of comparing yourself to others: It's important to remember that everyone is different, and comparing yourself to others is not healthy or productive. Accepting and embracing your individuality will help you feel better about yourself and boost your confidence.

8. Seek out support: If you're struggling with low self-confidence, seeking support from a therapist or a coach can be helpful. Talking about your feelings and getting guidance can help you feel better about yourself and improve your confidence.

9. Give yourself time: It takes time to build up your confidence, so don't expect to feel better about yourself overnight. Be patient and keep working on improving your self-confidence. The more you work at it, the better you feel about yourself.

10. Celebrate your accomplishments: When you accomplish something, big or small, take the time to celebrate it! Celebrating your accomplishments will help you feel good about yourself and boost your confidence levels.

By following these steps, you can start to feel better about yourself and boost your confidence levels. Remember, building up your self-confidence takes time and effort, but the result is worth it!

Top tips

- Go an extra mile and enjoy watching yourself grow.
- Don't try to cover up mistakes; learn from them to grow.
- Crash down the taboo of embarrassment by accepting compliments and learn to love yourself; just use the art of saying "thank you".
- Accept criticism and not react to the events of your childhood. Your past does not define your future.
- Visualise yourself doing great and confident. Adopt the way it looks, sounds, and feels.
- Confidence comes from learning to love and accept yourself.
- **Watch out for:** Internalising – Stewing over – becoming defensive – ignoring and hurting inside – running away – shutting down – anger & blame – confusion.
- You got this!

Weekly goals:

Set 1 intention each day this week.

Work on changing 1 limiting belief about yourself this week and look for evidence - opening up the RAS (Reticular Activating System).

Pick up 1 hobby that you used to enjoy or have been wanting to try for a long time.

Mind your self-narration & remember the power of words.

Write down 3 things that people like about you.

Write down 3 things that you are proud of about yourself.

Assertion and setting boundaries

Many people think that being assertive is the same as being aggressive. Assertion is about setting boundaries and red lines so others do not cross them. It is also fair to others to set our boundaries because if we do not communicate what is acceptable and what is not for us, there is no confusion, and the other person is clear on what you do not tolerate.

ACT - NOT REACT!

If we communicate our values and boundaries clearly with others, then it is easier to stand up for our rights when they cross the line. And if that is not good enough for them, well then perhaps a discussion might be needed about how much this person is adding to your life and the quality of the relationship.

No is the new "yes".

We all have basic rights, and it is unacceptable for others to try to violate them. In fact, you will find that people do like the clear lines because if we do not set them, firstly, we make ourselves vulnerable to our rights getting violated; secondly, it may be confusing for others. And let's admit, it is not fair to blame others for crossing our line when we have not set it clearly to start with.

Look at these communication styles, and maybe check out what your style might be as well as of the people you are close with or work with. What is their style? How do they communicate?

Communication styles

SORRY	**Passive Communication** I will meet your wants and needs; what I want and my needs are not met - violating my own rights	Always looking for approval, not taking the risk of confronting others about something we don't like. *"It is ok, no problem, we will do what you like, I don't mind, I am sorry, it is my fault"*. It creates resentment, frustration, and affects self-worth, causing low self-esteem and stress.
	Aggressive Communication I want my needs met, I don't care about your needs	It is all because of you; this is your fault; I want it this way, my way or high way. Forceful and ignores the rights of others, with no compromise. Uses put-downs, loud voices, criticises others, bullies, tries to dominate, demanding, and temperamental due to victim mode.
	Passive Aggressive Communication Accepting to meet your needs and dismissing my own needs and wants.	I will do what you want and need, but I will get you for this later. You will see. Expressing negative emotions indirectly by being cynical and hostile, silent treatment, and frequently complaining about not being appreciated. Indirect and dishonest, not giving the other person a fair chance to see the clear lines, and victim mode.
	Assertive Communication I am ok, you are ok, I accept my needs and your needs, let's negotiate.	Actively listening to the other person, being able to communicate your needs clearly and calmly, seeing the broader picture, from different perspectives, considerate of the rights of self as well as others, ok with compromise, respectful to self and others' rights.

Passive communication is difficult to spot easily by others because with aggressive, at least you can see what's going on. Passive communication is more about not wanting to do what the other person does, but you are submissive and accept to do what they want to do, with the fear that otherwise you might be rejected. Deep down, it is about fear of rejection and the desire to be liked, accepted and approved. In the long run, this communication style can cause resentment, anger and even sadness because you never look after your own needs. It is always about other people's needs being prioritised above your own.

It can result in frequent complaints about not being appreciated, but in fact, they're really not aware of what you want and need, so it is also unfair to other people when you are not communicating your wishes.

The aggressive communication style is about not wanting my needs met and not caring about what others need. I want everyone to do what I want: shouting, bullying, if necessary to get it your way, put-downs, loud voices, criticising others for not meeting your wants and needs. When you shout, you actually bully other people because you don't want to hear what they have to say.

The passive-aggressive style is about accepting other people's needs and wants, again, not communicating or vaguely communicating what you want, but deep inside, you resent doing so and even feel angry and frustrated, so you show this with behaviour. You might go to the cinema because the other person insists, even though you would rather go for dinner, but then in the cinema, you are resentful about being there, not talking and being grumpy, silent treatment and so on.

Assertive communication is more about clearly communicating your wants and needs, listening to the other person's wants and needs with an open mind, trying to see it from their perspective and negotiating and talking about it. You are okay, I am okay, here is what I would like, and I accept what you need; let's find a middle way.

There are some myths about assertive communication; some people think it is aggressive, but that is very far from what it is about. Assertion is about your own rights as a person, respecting and understanding the other person's rights, and negotiating peacefully. We have language to communicate and negotiate, which reminds me of a quote by Ludwig

Wittgenstein: "The limits of my language mean the limits of my world".

Being able to stand up for yourself assertively and communicating your needs openly improves your self-esteem, and setting clear lines helps avoid misunderstandings and improve relationships; it is a win/win for everyone.

When we are not assertive, we may find ourselves communicating in unhelpful ways. Let's have a look at communication styles and see if you recognise them in yourself and others.

Communication styles and power relations

Communication styles also affect power relations, and I think this is an important one. The power relations with a passive communicator always seeking approval, not taking risks, staying in the safe zone and not growing, is just giving away the power over you to others. You just keep trying to fulfil other people's needs, and you start getting frustrated and angry inside for taking them on and for people bringing them to you. You are not communicating that you have a problem with this and are letting yourself down by not looking after yourself.

The aggressive communicator is very straightforward; they will openly shout, scream and not listen to others, threaten, use the advantages they have over the other person to silence them until they claim power over others and control the other person's behaviour through bullying, belittling, embarrassing them in front of others and so on, so they get power through creating fear.

The passive-aggressive communicator might punish others by withdrawing love and affection or giving silent treatment if they don't get what they want. They might even get ill for not getting what they want, and others may feel guilty for causing this. *"It is your fault that I feel miserable or even ill"*. This type of communicator usually has the victim mindset, blaming others for how they feel. They do not recognise that their thoughts, emotions and behaviour are only in their control and responsibility, nobody else's. This type of communication can also be quite manipulative to others.

An assertive communicator has this personal power through accepting yourself, learning about yourself, growing, and being okay with being who you are. It is about being able to make your own choices rather than accepting what anybody else tells you to do, being dependent on other people and claiming that personal power is important for your self-esteem.

Passive communication: I meet your needs, but my needs are not met - violating my own rights - Gives away power. Always looking for approval, not taking the risk of confronting others about something we don't like. *"It is ok, no problem, we will do what you like, I don't mind, I am sorry, it is my fault"*. Unable to tell the boss that there are too many files coming in to work on and you are drowning in it or not telling friends that you cannot keep picking up their children from school every day.

Let's say you are out with a friend who suggests going to the cinema, but you actually want to go to a restaurant and have dinner. If you are a passive communicator, you will agree because meeting other people's needs is more important than your own.

Especially if you have low self-esteem and feel not good enough, fearing rejection and shame, you would most likely be saying yes to too many things, even though they're not suitable for you, and you don't want them. In order to avoid rejection, you might find yourself saying *"yes"* to things even when your needs and wants are unmet, which in the long run causes resentment, frustration, and stress and affects your self-worth.

One way is also to look for evidence for and against your predictions and test your assumptions. If you think people will not talk to you if you say *"no"*, then try to experiment and see what happens. More often than not, people find that when they say no, others usually just say, *"Okay, no problem"*, so it is worth testing out these assumptions.

Aggressive communication: I want my needs met; I don't care about your needs - Abusing power. Does not accept responsibility of own emotions and actions and projects the responsibility onto other people.

It is all because of you; this is your fault; I want it this way, my way or the highway. Forceful and ignores the rights of others, with no compromise. Uses put-downs, loud voice, criticises others, bullies, tries to dominate, demanding, temperamental.

Controlling others, punishing and abusing them, withdrawing love and affection when they don't do as we tell them or making them feel guilty that it is their fault we are not feeling well.

Passive aggressive communication: Accept to meet your needs, not mine, but I am resentful. - Misusing power

Ok, I will do what you need, but I will get you for this later. You will see.

Expressing negative emotions indirectly by being cynical and hostile, silent treatment, and frequently complaining about not being appreciated. Indirect and dishonest, not giving the other person a fair chance to see the clear lines.

Looking excessively after others, so they become dependent on us, emotional blackmail, or telling them we love them exactly as they are, and they must not change.

Assertive communication: I am ok, you are ok, I accept my needs and your needs – Assertive power

Actively listening to the other side, communicating your needs clearly and calmly, seeing the broader picture from different perspectives, being considerate of the rights of self and others, being okay with compromise, and being respectful to self and others' rights.

Power through finding yourself and being fine with being your authentic self. It is about making your own choices without being overly dependent and wanting the approval of others. Communicating assertively also positively affects self-esteem.

Power Relations

Passive: Gives away power	Always looking for approval, not taking the risk of confronting others about something we don't like. - Unable to tell the boss that too many files are coming in to sort and drowning in it, not telling friends that you cannot keep picking up their children from school every day.
Aggressive: Abusing power	Controlling others, punishing and abusing them, withdrawing love and affection when they don't do as we tell them or making them feel guilty that it is their fault we are not feeling well - You bring my blood pressure right up, you will be the end of me.
Passive Aggressive: Misusing power	Looking excessively after others, so they become dependent on us, emotional blackmail, or telling them we love them exactly as they are, and they must not change.
Assertive power	Power through finding yourself and being fine with being you. It is about making your own choices without being overly dependent and wanting the approval of others. Important for self-esteem.

Disadvantages of becoming assertive

If you have been passive, some people may not take it lightly that you start claiming your rights. As you claim your personal power, the person who may have been used to having more control previously may not be too impressed and may not want to lose their power.

It may result in losing some friends or family members who cannot accept your assertion and would rather you do as they think you should. Assertion may not always get you the desired result, and learning new ways and working with new beliefs, trying to let go of unhelpful ones takes extra effort and determination. But you will find your authentic self, self-acceptance, self-respect and self-love, which is the beginning of a long-lasting, happy relationship. This will also affect your relationship with others positively in the long run.

It is okay to take responsibility for our decisions because, remember, we do the best we can to make the best decision with what we have in our hands today. No one can yet see the future, so it may or may not turn out to be the most favourable, but imperfect action is better than perfect inaction.

Advantages of communication styles:

Passive
Others praise me for being selfless.
It is not my fault if things go wrong.
I don't like conflict, so I don't have to deal with it.
I don't feel guilty if I say yes.

Aggressive
I get what I want.
Others will fulfil my needs.
I feel powerful and in control rather than vulnerable.

Passive-aggressive
I feel temporary relief.
I feel powerful and satisfied.
I have control and show them when they are wrong.

Assertive
Being able to stand up for yourself improves your self-esteem.
You can communicate your needs momentarily in a calm matter and avoid building up resentment.
Setting clear lines helps avoid most misunderstandings.
Makes your loved ones feel listened to.
Improves relationships in the long run.

Negative beliefs about assertion
Assertion is the same as aggression.
I can get what I want if I am assertive.
Once I am assertive, I must always be assertive.

What can get in the way?
It is embarrassing to say what I want.
People will reject me if I say what I want.
If I give my opinion, they may argue with me.
The other person will get angry or upset with me.
I will ruin the relationship/friendship.
It is rude and selfish.

Are you setting limits and drawing boundaries, clarifying what we will do and accept and what we won't do and accept? Keeping vague boundaries can be confusing for other people and can cause misunderstanding as well as arguments.

When in doubt, refer to "Your Basic Human Rights" on the next page. Print it, hang it on the fridge, look at it, and take it in every day.

"YOUR BASIC RIGHTS" as a Human Being

- You have the right to say, "no."
- You have the right to change your mind.
- You have the right to make mistakes and use them as part of your growth.
- You have the right to look after yourself and put yourself first sometimes.
- You have the right to say, "I don't know."
- You have the right to be independent of the goodwill of others.
- You have the right to make mistakes and be responsible for them.
- You have the right to decide what is best for you without being judged by others.
- You have the right to say, "I don't understand."
- You have the right to do less than you are humanly capable of doing.
- You have the right to take the time you need to respond.
- You have the right to disagree with others regardless of their position or numbers.
- You have the right to feel all of your emotions (including anger) and express them *"appropriately"*.
- You have the right to ask questions.
- You have the right to be treated with respect.
- You have the right to ask for what you want and need.
- You have the right to feel good about yourself and your achievements.
- You have the right to choose when you do not wish to be responsible for finding solutions to other people's problems.
- You have the right to exercise any and all of these rights, without feeling guilty.

Top tips:

- Self-acceptance and authenticity are part of our growth, and a rigid outlook on ourselves always correlates with high levels of stress. Blaming ourselves for a decision made with what we know now, which we did not know in the past, is simply being unfair on ourselves.
- You are enough.
- Your journey is unique.
- Remind yourself that "self-worth" is not dependent on "success".
- What you may call a "failure" is actually a "bounce", which is necessary for personal growth and development.

How would an assertive person respond to criticism?

Notice perfectionism emotions, watch behaviours, let's break the habits.

What are the changes you want to start applying?

Mind Mastery:

Emotional Mastery:

Behavioural Mastery:

Chapter 8

Values: The Compass Within

Values are one of the most important building blocks of life. They make us feel good and bad when we don't live aligned with them. Values are about what we care about and hold dear to our hearts, our fundamental beliefs, and they determine our priorities, effect choices that give meaning to our lives.

They are very important for our sense of self, who we are, what we feel about ourselves, and the actions we take. Values are not an outcome but are continuous all through our lives. Let's say if friendship is very important for you, but you never call your friends, then you are not living aligned with this value. If you call them once, the value is not achieved and done. Values are not goals, but aligning our goals with our values gives satisfaction, contentment and motivation.

We have been discussing how we start forming our thoughts and beliefs about ourselves, others and the world from a very young age. Our values start forming along with those as well. Our values are an important part of what we hold dear in our lives, what really matters, what we take pride in, and ultimately guide how we spend our time and energy to get life satisfaction and fulfilment.

Values are our fundamental beliefs, which determine our priorities and life direction and help us make the choices that give meaning to our lives. Values are also important for our sense of self, and rather than being an outcome, they are continuous throughout life.

I guess you can say that they are the choices we make that bring meaning and inspiration to our lives, the things that matter to us. I separate those in terms of internal and external.

In the 21st century, we are more stressed than ever. As technology becomes more advanced to make life easier for us to have more time to do what we would like to do as humans, it seems we are becoming increasingly lost in them. More about this in the final chapter, "Searching for Happiness".

"Stress" has become a word that many people use almost daily. Often, we find ourselves under pressure and not living in harmony with our values, which can negatively impact how we view ourselves and our emotions. Finding a balance between things of high importance to us and how we live our daily lives matters.

After living and surviving in nature for thousands of years, we started separating ourselves from it by building huge cities with houses, flats, roads, workplaces and so on. Were we really born to live in the big cities, driving fast cars, or are we losing sight of our values? I remember seeing a programme about extremely rich people, and they got bigger private planes built, bigger yachts, and bought luxurious cars; yet, there was always someone else who had a better one or a bigger plane or a yacht.

If it is any consolation, it also turns out that most big prize lottery winners end up unhappy, many losing their friends and families breaking up. The people who seemed still happy several years after winning a large sum of money were those who were helping others, building schools in poor countries, and finding fulfilment in doing good for others once they had fulfilled their own needs.

What are the values? Think about the things that make your life more meaningful. Imagine how life would be without holding this value and how it would feel. We will rate them in the end, so the more it is important to you, the more emotions it would trigger, and hence, the higher the value.

Let's bring perfectionism in with the values. Perfectionism gives short-term gain, but the cost in the long term is high. Perhaps if we do not stop, take a step back and reflect on the cost, we may lead a whole life full of stress, anxiety, frustration, exhaustion, and even depression.

When we feel that we are not feeling okay, it is often because we are not aligned with our values. One of my clients, Annie, had been promoted to an executive-level management position, and she had started to put all her efforts, time and energy into her job. As a result, all other areas of her life had begun slipping. Every time a client was happy with a project, was the short-term gain, it felt good momentarily, but then she immediately had new projects to follow up on.

Annie started suffering from anxiety, especially Sunday nights felt awful with all physical sensations of anxiety with shallow breathing, heartbeat raising, hands shaking, and her stomach turning. She was feeling down because she could not understand why she felt this way. Annie told me that she was the main breadwinner in her family; she said she had a lovely family, they had a nice life, and in her high position, she should be strong and not feel weak like this. Feeling anxiety meant weakness for her, and weakness was unacceptable.

There are several limiting beliefs here; Annie's perfectionism in her professional life was taking all her time and energy for the price of all other areas in her life. She rarely saw her children or her husband during the week; she did not have any time to spend with her friends, nor was she able to make any time to look after herself and her needs. If a client decided to make changes in the project she and her team were working on, she took this personally, and she felt like a failure. She also called herself "weak", because she was feeling anxious.

We looked at Annie's wheel of life, and she rated the things that mattered the most to her. We then rated how much effort and energy she spends on these values that mean the most to her, and Annie realised that she was spending all her time and energy on her work, which mattered less than her husband and children, and she decided to make some changes.

Annie realised that she was not living her life aligned with her values and made vital changes that would secure her spending more time with her family. And she ended up making a new contract with her company to work for four days a week.

I once read about Steven Hayes' fantastic exercise and would like to share it with you. I think it puts values neatly into perspective. Just imagine someone describing you in two different ways at your funeral. One, you are afraid that they might; second, everything you would hope them to say. Are you living aligned with values that give meaning to your life?

Here are some main values in no particular order. Those values may also shift in different periods of your life. For example, you may change your outlook on intimate relationships or parenting in different stages of your life.

1 - Marriage – Intimate relationships

Think about how important it is for you to have a partner, or a significant other and what is important for you in a romantic relationship. You may or may not have an intimate relationship or be married at the moment; nevertheless, this is more about your opinion and what matters for you in a relationship.

What kind of a partner would you like to be, what would you like to be doing, how would you act towards your partner, and how would you treat your significant other? Think about the reasons behind these acts, your motivation to be the kind of partner that matters to you, and the kind of relationship you would like to cultivate.

Perfectionist thinking examples:

-I must be the perfect partner and always ensure my partner is happy.

-We must be the perfect couple and never have disagreements. Any disagreements make me question the compatibility and success of the relationship.

-He should be giving me flowers or presents and texting me back immediately if he loves me.

- If my partner doesn't meet all of my expectations and perfectly fulfils my needs, then they are not the right person for me.

- I fear that my partner's imperfections reflect poorly on me as a judge of character. I worry about being judged by others based on my partner's appearance, achievements, or behaviour.

- I constantly seek reassurance and validation from my partner to feel secure in the relationship. I rely on their approval to validate my self-worth and feel anxious if it is not consistently provided.

Remember, we all have different love languages. Some of us like receiving presents, for others it could be about intimacy or service. I definitely recommend the book "The 5 Love Languages" by Dr Gary Chapman.

The five love languages concept, "words of affirmation, acts of service, receiving gifts, quality time, and physical touch," is about how we like to give and receive love. If you and your partner speak different languages, it can be like speaking Spanish and Dutch, but still trying to understand each other.

2 – Core Family

Think of your immediate family: your parents, cousins, aunts, uncles, nephews, nieces, etc. What kind of a son or daughter, uncle, auntie, or grandchild would you like to be? What matters for you in these relationships? What are the reasons behind how you would like to act, how you would like to treat them, and how you want to be treated by them?

This can be modelled or perceived as perfectionism, trying to be the perfect daughter/son, cousin, or sibling. Perception of the parents' high expectations or learned perfectionism because the parents only show affection when there are high-level achievements. Perfect or failure, no grey area between.

It can also become problematic when we have other-oriented perfectionism. Our expectations from other family members did not live up to our high standards.

Perfectionist thinking examples:

-I must always drop everything and fulfil my parents' or other family members' needs at all costs.
-I have difficulty accepting my family members' individuality and flaws. I believe they should meet certain expectations, and I often find myself disappointed when they don't live up to those standards.
- My family must always appear happy, successful, and perfect to the outside world. Any signs of imperfection or dysfunction reflect poorly on me.
- I have difficulty accepting my family members' individuality and flaws. I believe they should meet certain expectations, and I often find myself disappointed when they don't live up to those standards.

3 - Parenthood

Once we have children, parenthood usually becomes a huge priority. You may not have children but still may have ideas about how much parenthood matters to you. What are the most important things about being a parent, what does it mean, and what is the motivation behind your ideas of "the perfect parent" if such a thing exists, which is fair to say it doesn't?

Perfectionist thinking examples:

If your children are having problems, we blame ourselves for not being a good enough parent.
- I must be the perfect mother or I am a failure, and my children will suffer.
- I must be the perfect parent, always knowing what to do and making the right decisions. Any mistakes or missteps I make reflect my inadequacy as a parent.
- I must always give the perfect advice to my children
- I should make sure my children are never unhappy
- If my child does not get great grades, it is my fault, I have not done my job as a parent.
- I constantly worry that I am not doing enough for my children. I feel the need to constantly provide them with the perfect environment, experiences, and opportunities to ensure their success.

Remember that perfection is unattainable, and striving for it can lead to stress and burnout. Focus on being a loving and supportive parent rather than an unattainably perfect one. Embrace imperfections as valuable learning opportunities for both you and your children. It's through mistakes and challenges that growth and resilience are fostered.

Cultivate open communication with your children and create an environment where they feel comfortable expressing their thoughts, feelings, and concerns without fear of judgment. Allow your children the space to explore their interests and passions, even if they differ from your expectations or preferences. And last but not least, encourage them to pursue their own paths, love and support them *unconditionally*.

4 - Friendship

When it comes to friendships, you may have these incredibly high expectations for yourself and others. You feel this constant pressure to be the perfect friend, always being available, understanding, and attentive to everyone's needs. It's like you are afraid of falling short or letting your friends down.

And guess what? You also have really high standards for your friends, expecting them to always be reliable, supportive, and in tune with your emotions. It can be tough for you to accept any imperfections or conflicts in friendships because you see them as personal failures or signs of incompatibility.

What does friendship mean to you? What qualities would you like to offer in your friendships, and what are the building blocks of a friendship for you? Also, think about what qualities people need before you can call them friends and what your expectations are from your friends.

Perfectionist thinking examples:

If you are a perfectionist, you will most likely always be checking your performance as a friend, and perhaps your friends' performance as well, to measure whether it is in accordance with your high expectations.

- I must always say yes to my friends, or they will be disappointed and reject me.
- They should always be answering my text straight away, or it means they don't care about me.
- If I can't always be there for my friends or meet their needs perfectly, then I'm failing as a friend.
- I constantly worry about whether I'm doing enough for my friends and meeting their expectations. Any perceived shortcomings make me feel guilty and inadequate.
- I expect my friends to always be available and attentive to my needs, just as I strive to be for them. Any signs of them being less-than-perfect friends make me question the strength of our relationship.
- I worry that my friends will judge me if they see any flaws or mistakes in my actions or decisions. I fear that any imperfections might cause them to distance themselves or view me differently.
- I put pressure on myself to always say the right things, offer the perfect advice, and provide unwavering support. I struggle to accept that it's okay to make mistakes or not have all the answers.

It's understandable that this pursuit of perfection can create stress and strain in your friendships. I believe it is important to embrace the imperfections, both in ourselves and in others, and to create a space of acceptance and understanding rather than aiming for an unattainable idea of a perfect friendship.

5 - Work/Employment

When it comes to work life, sometimes you might have these incredibly high expectations from yourself and others. You might put a lot of pressure on yourself to achieve perfection in everything you do. You might also be setting exceedingly high standards and expect flawless performance from yourself. You might believe that anything less than perfection is a personal failure. Not only that, but you also have these high expectations of your colleagues or your team, expecting them to meet the same level of perfection and dedication.

Have a think about what your professional life means to you and why. How important is it for you to be successful? Is this the same as doing everything at work perfectly? This area is quite common, where perfectionists often set much time and energy. Having goals and wanting to strive is good. We are given this life as a gift to contribute; however, getting every job you apply for or never making mistakes at work is not sustainable or humanly possible.

Perfectionist thinking examples:

- I must always make the right decisions, leading to the best outcomes.

- If I don't achieve perfect results in my work, it means I'm not competent or valuable as an employee.
- I constantly worry about making mistakes or not meeting deadlines. Any minor error or setback feels like a personal failure.
- I put immense pressure on myself to excel in every aspect of my work. Anything less than perfection leaves me feeling dissatisfied and anxious."
- I fear criticism or feedback from colleagues or superiors, as I perceive it as a reflection of my inadequacy or incompetence.
- I struggle to delegate tasks or ask for help because I believe that I should be able to handle everything flawlessly on my own.

Sorry to break you the news, but there are 7.9 billion people on Earth, and none of them are flawless. It is important to remember that nobody is perfect, and striving for perfection can lead to unnecessary stress and anxiety. Embracing imperfections, finding a healthy work-life balance, and recognising that excellence can be achieved without absolute perfection can make your work life more enjoyable and fulfilling.

6 - Physical wellbeing

What does your physical well-being, your health mean to you? As a perfectionist, you might have a unique physical well-being perspective, driven by your relentless pursuit of flawlessness and excellence in every aspect of your life. Physical wellbeing is not just about maintaining a healthy body but also about achieving an ideal state of physical perfection. You would strive to attain the perfect physique, meticulously sculpted through rigorous exercise, strict dieting, and a dedication to maintaining a flawless appearance.

Perfectionist thinking examples:

-I must always have the perfect weight, the perfect body.
-If I don't have a perfectly toned body, I am unattractive and unworthy of love and acceptance.
-Every flaw or imperfection on my body is a sign of personal failure. I need to constantly strive for flawless physical beauty.
-I can't enjoy social events or wear certain clothes unless my body looks absolutely perfect. I must constantly monitor and control my appearance to avoid judgment or criticism.

It is essential to find a balance between striving for excellence and maintaining a healthy perspective on your body. Embracing self-compassion, setting realistic goals, and focusing on overall well-being rather than external appearances can help you develop a healthier relationship with your physical self.

By appreciating your body for what it can do rather than solely focusing on how it looks, you can find a more sustainable and fulfilling approach to physical well-being. Think about your legs; do they take you where you want to go? Do your hands help you grab and carry things or write? Do your eyes see what is around you? If they are functioning well, then consider yourself blessed.

7 - Personal growth/Education

Self-growth is a lifelong journey that allows individuals to continuously evolve, discover their strengths, and work on their weaknesses. It promotes self-awareness, personal fulfilment, and a sense of purpose, enabling individuals to lead meaningful and enriched lives. The personal value of education and self-growth lies in their ability to nurture personal growth, foster self-confidence, and unlock the potential for lifelong learning and fulfilment.

Now have a think about how you would like to grow, what is important for you to know and learn more about and why. Where does it lie in your overall values as a person? Below you can find some examples of a perfectionist thinking about personal growth and education, which would cause putting pressure on yourself, and missing the benefits of self-growth.

Perfectionist thinking examples:

- I place immense value on self-growth and education because I believe they are crucial for achieving success and staying ahead in a competitive world. Anything less feels like falling behind.

-I constantly compare myself to others who are more educated or seem to be progressing faster in their self-growth journey. It makes me question my own worth and pushes me to constantly strive for more.

- I have a tendency to be overly critical of myself when it comes to self-growth and education. I constantly push myself to achieve more and often feel guilty or inadequate if I don't meet my own high standards.

When it comes to your value of self-growth and education as a perfectionist, it's important to find a balance. While it's commendable to have high aspirations and a drive for excellence, remember that self-growth is a journey, not a destination. Embrace the process and allow yourself to make mistakes and learn from them. Recognise that self-worth isn't solely determined by external achievements or comparing yourself to others. Cultivate self-compassion and celebrate your progress along the way.

8 - Community/Citizenship

Being an active member of a community and fulfilling the responsibilities of citizenship contribute to a sense of belonging, connection, and purpose. Engaging with and supporting one's community fosters social bonds, empathy, and cooperation, creating a shared sense of identity and collective well-being.

What would being involved in your community mean to you and why? How important is it for you to be a part of it?

Perfectionist thinking examples:

-I believe that I must be the perfect citizen and community member, always volunteering, attending meetings, and actively engaging in initiatives. Anything less makes me feel like I'm not doing enough for the greater good.

-I constantly compare myself to others who seem to be more involved in their communities or advocating for social causes. It creates a constant sense of pressure to prove my commitment and dedication to citizenship.

-I often find it hard to balance my personal and community responsibilities. I struggle with the guilt of not dedicating enough time or resources to all.

-I place immense pressure on myself to make a significant impact on my community and society as a whole. I feel a constant need to go above and beyond, striving for perfection in all my efforts.

-I should be doing more for my community but I struggle to find the time to give back, which makes me feel constantly guilty.

If you relate to any of the sentences above, think about the ways of finding a balance between your personal responsibilities and your community engagements, prioritising self-care. Appreciate the value of small acts and celebrate progress, understanding that every individual effort counts. Lastly, practice self-compassion and embrace the lifelong journey of community involvement and citizenship, learning and growing along the way.

9 - Money/Finance

The personal value of money and finance varies from individual to individual. For some, financial security and stability are essential values that provide a sense of peace and freedom. Others may prioritise financial independence, using money as a means to achieve their goals and dreams. Money can also be valued as a tool for creating opportunities, supporting loved ones, and making a positive impact in the world through charitable contributions. Ultimately, the value of money and finance lies in its ability to provide a sense of control, flexibility, and the ability to make choices that align with one's values and aspirations.

Have a think about where money and finance stand amongst your values. How does it factor into your personal values and beliefs, and how does it influence your decision-making, relationships, and overall sense of fulfilment in life?

Perfectionist thinking examples:

- I must constantly strive for financial success and wealth to prove my worth and competence.
- Any financial setback or failure reflects directly on my abilities and makes me feel like a failure as a person.
- I need to meticulously track and control every penny I spend to ensure I am making the most optimal financial choices.
- I feel a constant pressure to compare myself to others and their financial achievements, fearing that I am falling behind or not measuring up.

You are so many things to so many people, and your worth as a person extends far beyond your financial success. Practice self-compassion and challenge the idea of perfection, acknowledging that setbacks and failures are part of the learning process. Focus on your own financial goals and values rather than comparing yourself to others. Allow yourself to enjoy the fruits of your labour without guilt, finding a balance between saving and spending.

10 - Spirituality

Spirituality provides a framework for understanding the deeper aspects of life and the universe, offering solace, guidance, and a sense of purpose. It allows individuals to tap into their inner wisdom, cultivate compassion, and foster a greater sense of gratitude and interconnectedness. Nurturing spirituality can lead to personal growth, self-discovery, and a deeper understanding of oneself and the world, contributing to a more balanced, harmonious, and fulfilling existence.

Have a think about where spirituality stands amongst your values. How does spirituality factor into your personal values and beliefs, and how does it influence your decision-making, relationships, and overall sense of fulfilment in life?

Perfectionist thinking examples:

-I fear that if I don't have a deep and profound spiritual experience, I'm somehow lacking in my faith or spirituality.
-I often compare myself to others who seem to have stronger connections, which diminishes my own sense of worth.

- I tend to judge myself harshly when it comes to my spirituality, believing that any misstep or lack of discipline reflects a personal failing.
- I often feel guilty if I can't dedicate as much time or energy to my spiritual practices as I believe I should.

To those who struggle with perfectionism in their spirituality, I offer a gentle reminder: spirituality is a deeply personal and evolving journey. Embrace the beauty of imperfection and release the need for rigid standards or comparisons. Allow yourself the freedom to explore and discover your own unique path without the burden of constantly striving for perfection.

Remember that spirituality is about connection, growth, and finding meaning in your own way. Be gentle with yourself, cultivate self-compassion, and find joy in the process rather than fixating on the destination. Embrace authenticity, listen to your inner voice, and trust that your spiritual journey is valid and worthy, no matter how it may differ from others.

11 - Recreation/Hobbies

Engaging in recreational activities and pursuing hobbies allows for a much-needed break from the demands of daily life, promoting relaxation, stress relief, and overall well-being. They provide a space for personal expression, creativity, and self-discovery, allowing individuals to explore their passions and interests outside of work or responsibilities.

Recreation and hobbies also foster a sense of accomplishment, as progress and mastery are often experienced in these endeavours. They contribute to a balanced lifestyle, bringing joy, fulfilment, and a sense of purpose, ultimately enhancing one's overall quality of life.

Have a think about where recreation and hobbies stand amongst your values. How does recreation and hobbies factor into your personal values and beliefs, and how does it influence your decision-making, relationships, and overall sense of fulfilment in life?

Perfectionist thinking examples:

-I have a hard time indulging in hobbies because I feel the need to be the best or achieve perfection in everything I do.
-It's challenging for me to embrace leisure without feeling like I should be doing something more meaningful or productive.
-I find it difficult to relax and fully immerse myself in recreational activities because my perfectionistic tendencies make me hyper-focused on the end result or outcome.
-I tend to compare myself to others in my hobbies, constantly seeking validation or reassurance that I am 'good enough' or 'better' than others.

Remember that recreational activities and hobbies are meant to bring joy, relaxation, and personal fulfilment. Release the need for constant achievement or comparison. Embrace the process and journey rather than fixating solely on the end result or performance. Give yourself permission to explore and engage in activities simply for the sake of enjoyment, without attaching expectations or judgments.

The wheel of life

We all would like to have happiness, contentment and success. Whether it's professionally or in our private lives, aligning our values with our goals is vital to achieve this.

The wheel of life helps us understand and reflect upon our values, which then helps us take the steps we need in order to live aligned with them. It helps us clarify and understand the discrepancies between our values and how we live our lives so we can re-adjust our goals towards happiness, contentment and success.

Have a look at some of the main values identified by people and think about what they mean to you. Rate them as you go. If there are any values that are not mentioned here, there are a couple of empty ones at the end for you to fill in and put the reasons why.

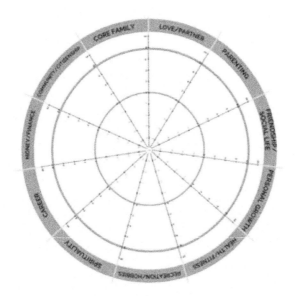

GFX created by Rhea Monte

Take a moment to rate each area as you feel they are at the moment.

Rate each of them as of the current day.

-10 is as bad as it gets, 0 not good, +10 is fantastic, and it cannot get any better.

Take your time to do so.

Draw a line to show where you have rated that area of your life.

Now look at each area again

What number would you like each to be?

Are there any discrepancies between the numbers as they are today and what number you would like them to be?

What needs to happen to change this?

I think as we go through life, our priorities can shift and change, and that's also normal. In different stages of life, perhaps every decade, our values kind of move and shift. Sometimes, some things become more important than others.

The wheel of life helps us understand what is really important, to stop and reflect upon them, identify if the way we live our life and values are aligned, help us see the discrepancies, and then take the steps we need to align with them.

Top tips about values

- Find activities that suit your values.
- Your needs and your interests matter for your happiness and meaning in your life.
- Take time for exercise or hobbies and turn off your phone perhaps for a period of time.
- Be mindful of the present moment.
- When you are not feeling well, check if you are aligned with your values.

- Be authentic and true to your values, even when faced with challenges or societal pressures.
- Values can evolve and change over time as you grow and gain new experiences. Embrace the opportunity for personal growth and be willing to re-evaluate and adjust your values as necessary.

Weekly Goals and Values Planner of a Perfectionist

1 – The values I will work on this week are:

_____

because,

_____

2 – The 2 goals I have for this week are:

-
-

Because they will bring me closer to my bigger goal of_____

My negative inner critique says…: _____

(I.e.,, I am not good enough, I am a failure, others are always happier, I can never do anything right, I am not as worthy as others, etc. just choose 1)

… and my intention this week is to look for evidence that proves the exact opposite.

The evidence I found:

_____

_____

I will do a Mindfulness exercise _____ **times this week.**

I am grateful for _____**, and I will remember to appreciate this daily this week.**

You can download free ebooks, worksheets, audio-guided meditation and attention training at https://www.mindandmood.co.uk/resources/

Chapter 9

Heart and Mind Aligned:
Self- Compassion and Mindfulness

T his chapter is all about the ways that will help with self-acceptance through self-compassion and be able to appreciate what we have right here right now, rather than living in the past or in the future, missing out on the *"precious now"*.

Self-compassion is the practice of treating yourself with kindness, understanding, and acceptance, especially during challenging times or when facing personal shortcomings. It involves offering yourself the same care and compassion you would extend to a dear friend or a loved one.

Mindfulness is the state of being fully present and aware in the present moment, without judgment or attachment to thoughts or emotions. It involves observing your thoughts and sensations with a sense of curiosity and non-reactivity, fostering a greater understanding of yourself and the world around you. The combination of self-compassion and mindfulness can create a powerful foundation for self-awareness, emotional well-being, and personal growth.

What is compassion?

In the heart of our shared human experience lies a core principle, an emotion that threads our collective narratives together: compassion. Compassion, in its purest essence, is an amalgamation of caring, soothing, and encouraging qualities.

It helps us fine-tune to pay attention to the cues of those in distress.

Emphasis on:
- Awareness, being attentive to the pain
- Normalising - we are not alone in feeling the pain
- Kindness, warmth and care for the pain, rather than ignoring
- Comforting and caring actions to reduce the pain

What is self-compassion?

While compassion is about others, self-compassion is directly for ourselves. We humans are very good at showing a lot of compassion and understanding to others, but it is usually a different story if it is about ourselves, especially if you are a perfectionist.

Self-compassion involves treating yourself with kindness, understanding, and acceptance, recognising that imperfections and mistakes are part of being human. It fosters a sense of inner support and nurturance.

In contrast, self-criticism involves being harsh, judgmental, and unforgiving towards oneself, often magnifying perceived flaws or shortcomings. It creates a negative internal dialogue that can diminish self-esteem and motivation.

Cultivating self-compassion involves practicing self-kindness, acknowledging that you are only human, and embracing mindfulness.

Challenging self-criticism, on the other hand, requires developing awareness, confronting negative thoughts, and replacing them with more compassionate and realistic ones.

Self-criticism vs.	Self-compassion
Thinking styles: Labelling - Should and must thinking – overgeneralising. I am such an idiot. I am so useless. I am pathetic. I should have got the promotion. I should have known better. Others are always better/happier/worthy. I will never get things right. I will never manage to have a relationship. No one likes me.	I am good enough as I am; I can only do my best. I will learn from this and look for the promotion again next time. I didn't know then; what I know now. There is a story behind every closed door; everyone has their own struggles. I may or may not work, at least I try. I am worthy of love. Some people like me, some don't and that's ok.
What does your critical self say and how does it make you feel? **What are your beliefs about self-criticism?**	**What are your beliefs about self-compassion?** **If you practice criticising yourself, you get really good at self-criticism,** **if you practice compassion, you become really good at compassion.**

I am a strong believer in the benefits of self-compassion, and I promote this daily with my clients as well. It is amazing how many of my clients are surprised when we start talking about self-compassion, realising how long they have been unkind to themselves.

I think self-compassion lies in the essence of self-acceptance and self-love, which can help transform your inner critical voice to be more positive and flexible, rather than the rigid standards set especially by a perfectionist.

According to Paul Gilbert (2010), we have three emotion regulation systems. One of them is about safety and threats focused. The activation of the amygdala and hypothalamus means we are in fight or flight in times of being in danger or perceiving danger. That happens when we are angry, disgusted, anxious or panicking.

The second regulation system is about drive, wanting, and pursuing. This is the system that is active when we would like to do better, get better marks, learn a new language, and the desire for success. It is also this part that drives "I want more" money, better cars, bigger houses and so on.

The third system is safeness and kindness, the soothing system, which is really the compassionate system. If those three systems are not in balance, we will start having issues one way or another. If it's just constant drive and want, there's a problem. If it is constantly feeling under threat, constantly feeling anxiety or anger, there's a problem.

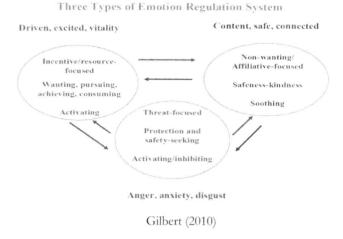

Three Types of Emotion Regulation System

Driven, excited, vitality

Content, safe, connected

Incentive/resource-focused

Wanting, pursuing, achieving, consuming

Activating

Non-wanting/Affiliative-focused

Safeness-kindness

Soothing

Threat-focused

Protection and safety-seeking

Activating/inhibiting

Anger, anxiety, disgust

Gilbert (2010)

The soothing system, along with compassion and kindness from others, helps calm down the threat and drive systems. Self-compassion will help in using the soothing system whenever needed.

Gilbert has suggested that too much of any of the systems are unhelpful and that there should be a fine balance. If we are just soothing ourselves in luxury and not doing anything, just indulging with no purpose, we have no drive and we have no threats, we then start feeling bored, useless, because there are no challenges, and as humans, we thrive with challenges to grow.

Would you feel sad and anxious if someone was constantly telling you that you are stupid, useless, or not good enough every time you did or said something that did not turn out to be the most favourable outcome?

You would start believing them over time because remember what you say to yourself in your head; you are also listening. I think I would be really sad to be listening to the non-stop critical voice inside my head. So, we really need to activate the soothing system within ourselves, the kindness towards ourselves as we would be to our loved ones. If it is not okay to say it to someone you love, then it is not okay to say it to yourself.

If you are hurting, be attentive to that pain, and remember that we are not alone. We all have our own stories of loss, rejection, and sadness. Everybody, at some point in their lives, feels that pain, feels sad and faces challenges. Nothing stays the same; everything keeps changing; the seasons, our bodies, the earth, the economy. Change is inevitable.

You may have made a decision in the past that perhaps did not turn out favourable. A perfectionist would wallow in regret, guilt and self-blame. Remember; you made a decision with the best of your abilities with the options you had then. It is unfair to judge your past self with what you know now. Because now you are in the future and you have experienced the outcome, which may not be favourable, but it for sure helped you learn and grow.

Self-compassion is about being able to soothe and comfort yourself. It's the direct opposite of self-criticism. If we look at self-criticism, some of you might recognise this, because the perfectionists are great at this, they are so good at criticising themselves. If you refer back to the **Unhelpful Thinking Habits**, there would be *"labelling, should and must"* thinking. And perhaps even *overgeneralising*?

You might hear yourself saying, "I'm such an idiot", "I'm so useless", or "I am pathetic," which is with labelling. "I should have got that promotion, I should have known better", which is "should and must thinking", and I must always help others no matter what the cost is for me. And then there is minimising and maximising under overgeneralising; "others are always better, happier, worthy, more deserving". What does your critical self say? And how does that make you feel?

What would you say to a loved one, a close friend or your child if they were feeling worthless, unlovable and stupid? Would you say "Yes, you are", or would you put on your loving kindness hat on, and try to make it better for them, soothe them?

Many people turn to me and say, "No, I would never say that!". I find this striking and just wondering, if you would never say that to someone you love and care about, what makes it okay to say to yourself, have a reflection on that one. You would show compassion and the wording you use to make them feel better would be very different. How about applying this for yourself? Remember, what you practice grows stronger.

If you practice self-compassion, you get really good at self-compassion. If you practice worrying, you get really good at worrying. If you practice criticising yourself constantly, you get really good at critical self. I think, now established, that is one of the reasons for depression and anxiety.

Emotions can be tricky, they are energy in motion, creating the way you feel and *"where your focus goes, energy flows"* says Tony Robbins. Building a positive set of feelings step by step; just enjoying a cup of tea, breathing the fresh air and being mindful of how you feel at that very moment, noticing how that feels in your body, and just being understanding of those feelings, and compassionate about how you feel. This too will pass, nothing is static; everything is in constant movement, evolving, shifting and changing, so are our feelings, and the situations.

If you are feeling really angry, it's okay, because anger is a basic emotion and helps us deal with situations, when we feel unfairly treated, we stand up for ourselves. Anger becomes a problem and unproductive, if we start shouting, throwing and smashing things, and slamming the doors. We do not get to communicate the real problem by doing these.

Take the responsibility to control your thoughts and emotions – remember emotion is energy in motion – and the behaviour that follows. You will find that those are habits, years and years of habits, a cycle you have been repeating for a long time. The good news is, by gaining awareness and wanting to change because it is no longer serving you, you have the ability to do so.

By gaining awareness, I mean telling yourself, "I can watch this, I can have a look at this feeling, I am not ashamed of it, or I don't need to escape it". Have a think about that thought that brought up the negative feeling. Then stay with that feeling, have a look at it, have a think about it. Take your time to understand and explore yourself.

Be careful how you speak to yourself, because how we communicate with ourselves and the words we use, shape our lives.

Emotions can be tricky - we may get angry about getting anxious, ashamed of losing our temper. This can get confusing. Soothing systems can be helpful and reduce attacking ourselves.

Learning to be kind and understanding to ourselves, building up positive feelings step by step, enjoying a cup of tea, breathing the fresh air, a nice hot shower and so on.

Remember, what you think to be a flaw, might be someone else's treasure.

Mindfulness

Mindfulness is a powerful tool for developing self-compassion and can be an incredibly rewarding journey. Mindfulness helps us to slow down and pay attention to our thoughts, feelings and physical sensations in the present moment without judgment. This allows us to become more aware of our triggers and reactions that lead to difficult emotions such as ***fear, anger, guilt or sadness***. It also helps us cultivate kindness, patience and acceptance towards ourselves which are key components of self-compassion.

The Mindfulness roadmap consists of several steps to help you build your capacity for mindful awareness. *The first step* involves learning how to recognise when we are in autopilot mode - where we are not paying attention – which we do a lot and developing the skills to bring ourselves back into a mindful state. Have you ever driven from one place to another without noticing how you got there?

Research by Harvard psychologists Matthew A. Killingsworth and Daniel T. Gilbert indicated that 47% of the time people's minds are wandering rather than paying attention to what they are doing. We either dwell on past events, "Why did I do this, why didn't I do that? How dare they do this to me, should I have made a different decision?" etc., or we worry about the future, "What if this happens, what if that happens, which means half of our lives, we are actually not in the present moment! Half! That is an incredible waste of a currency that we cannot exchange or buy again, "time".

Through practice, we can learn how to better observe our thoughts, feelings, physical sensations and interpretations of situations without getting caught up in them or making judgments about them.

Mindfulness Roadmap

The second step on the Mindfulness Roadmap is learning how to create space between ourselves and reactive thoughts or emotions by simply noticing them as they arise without attaching any meaning or judgment. Remember the automatic thoughts we looked at in Chapter 4. Once we are aware of the types of thoughts, it becomes easier to catch them before we have an emotional reaction.

This allows us to gain perspective on our experiences so that we can respond instead of reacting impulsively from a place of emotion rather than reasoning by using the thinking part of our brain, the cortex, rather than the emotional part of the brain, amygdala in the limbic brain.

The third step is cultivating kindness towards ourselves by recognising the shared human experience that all people feel pain and suffering at times. Mindful self-compassion involves allowing these painful feelings while also sending kindness towards ourselves with words like "It's okay" or "I understand" rather than punishing words like "You should have done this better" or "You should not have done this at all". Mindful self-compassion allows us to accept our flaws, forgive our mistakes and move forward with greater understanding and wisdom rather than being trapped in shame or guilt-based cycles.

The fourth step on the Mindfulness roadmap is practicing self-care through activities such as exercise, eating well, getting enough sleep, taking time for relaxation activities such as yoga or meditation, engaging in enjoyable activities that bring joy into your life and surrounding yourself with supportive relationships that strengthen your sense of belonging and connection.

These activities can help boost resilience levels so that you are better able to cope with everyday stressors without resorting back into autopilot mode, where it is easy for old patterns of behaviour associated with negative thinking to emerge again unbidden. Yoga is not a practice only for your physical well-being, but it also strengthens your mind.

Finally, *the fifth step* on the Mindfulness Roadmap involves finding ways to cultivate compassion for others by understanding their struggles as well as our own through empathy and expressing gratitude for all aspects of life, both large and small, that bring joy into our lives every day. This helps us stay connected with ourselves while nurturing connections with those around us, which can result in more meaningful personal and professional relationships, which enhances overall wellbeing even further over time when practiced consistently on a daily basis over long periods.

In summary, Mindfulness is an essential tool in cultivating self-compassion, which is essentially about treating oneself kindly even if things don't always go according to your expectations or plans, no matter what may come along life's journey throughout each day ahead. By engaging in the practices by following the Mindfulness Roadmap, you will be able to increase your concentration ability to be in the present moment, increasing awareness to be kind not only towards those around you but also yourself.

A vast amount of research shows that doing a relaxing activity or hobby mindfully, being in the moment, and paying attention has doubled the benefits. Just focusing on the present moment turns out to be the most beneficial while doing an activity you enjoy, i.e. yoga, gardening, walking, even being mindful when you have your tea or coffee, noticing the texture of the cup, the heat, the taste.

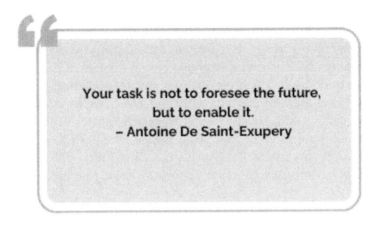

**Your task is not to foresee the future,
but to enable it.
- Antoine De Saint-Exupery**

When I started becoming interested in Mindfulness, I watched a TEDx talk with Dr. Shauna Shapiro, which affected me deeply. Dr Shapiro mentioned her first time in a monastery in Thailand and her first experiences of meditation.

She mentioned that during some of the first meditation sessions, she was thinking, "I don't belong here; I can't even figure out how to meditate; I am useless at this". She then found herself thinking, "What are these monks doing anyway? Don't they have anything else to do?". She talked about this with a monk, and the monk told her, "You are not practicing meditation; you are practicing judgement" he said those amazing words that always stayed with me:

"What you practice grows stronger."

It brings us to the beginning of the book when I talked about the neural pathways, how we learn, and how we get really good at things that we practice by strengthening those pathways so they become automatic.

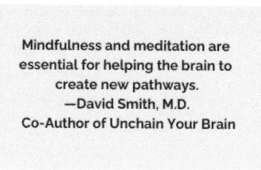

Mindfulness and meditation are
essential for helping the brain to
create new pathways.
—David Smith, M.D.
Co-Author of Unchain Your Brain

Just remember, not only paying attention, but paying kind attention.

When you notice your thoughts are wandering off to the future worries or dwelling about the past, remind yourself to come back and notice the present moment. Practicing this will really help to gain the mastery of your mind. Luckily, we can practice mindfulness anywhere and anytime. We can be mindful of the moment when our children are around us, or when we are having dinner with our family, or even on the bus.

On BBC2, Dr. Michael Mosley conducted an experiment to assess the impact of hobbies and mindfulness on reducing stress. The results showed that participating in hobbies and activities you enjoy, and especially mindfulness can significantly improve stress levels. Mindfulness stood out as the most effective stress-reducing approach in their experiment. As an example, I will use gardening; if you enjoy gardening, but while gardening you are also thinking about the report that you need to finish at work, or your shopping list, or what to cook for this evening, you are not getting the full benefit of that moment.

Here is a tip: Bring your mind back to the moment from wherever it may be while gardening, noticing how warm or cold the soil feels, how the sun feels on your skin, what you can smell, what you see and what you hear can help you feel happier and more relaxed by being fully in that moment with your mind, your body and your soul.

We often end up going back to the arms of nature, for nature to nurture us, and it always has a way of opening its arms and taking care of us.

I would like to share a Cherokee Wisdom Legend that I watched on YouTube about two wolves. One day, an elderly and wise Cherokee sits down with his grandson and tells about the war inside of all of us between two wolves.

One of the wolves is evil, full of jealousy, anger, ego, self-pity, resentment and arrogance.

The other wolf is good, full of love, peace, kindness, empathy, compassion for self and others, truth, hope, faith and generosity.

The wise elderly Cherokee says to his grandson that this war happens inside his heart and inside his grandson's, every woman's, man's and child's hearts. The grandson takes a moment to think about it and asks, "Which wolf will win?" The grandfather answers, *"The one you feed".*

Which wolf will *you* feed?

You can find the full version of this legend on the link below:
https://www.youtube.com/watch?v=x95_BTeanI8

How to Meditate Regularly

| Make yourself comfortable. | Start with just 3 minutes and increase it slowly. | Find the right time and commit to it. | Try using a meditation app or podcast as a guide. | Don't expect immediate results -- just keep at it. |

You can also chose to do an activity you like "Mindfully", be present, and notice.

Understanding meditation and mindfulness

-Mindfulness supports and enriches meditation, and meditation nurtures and expands mindfulness.

-Meditation is a practice, and using this practice, it can be possible to develop different qualities, including mindfulness.

-Meditation is usually practiced for a specific amount of time. Mindfulness is the quality of being able to pay kind attention to the present time and can be practiced anytime, anywhere.

-Mindfulness and concentration are two components of many meditation practices.

Benefits of mindfulness

A wealth of new research has been explored and found that Mindfulness practice can help:

-Reduce rumination.

-Feeling better, happier and calmer.

-Boost working memory.

-Lower blood pressure.

-Improves the digestion system.

-Decrease stress, anxiety and depression.

-Reduces tension around pain.

-Increase focus.

-Reduce emotional reactivity.

-Improve sleep.
-Cognitive flexibility.
-Promotes cultivating mindfulness, reducing stress, and enjoying the pleasures of everyday life.

"Put your thoughts on the birds and watch them fly" exercise ©

Find a comfortable place to sit down and relax. Take a few deep breaths as you close your eyes. I would like you to think about beautiful birds in a row as they fly. Keep breathing and watching them.

Take a deep breath all the way down to your diaphragm and breathe out. As you go back to your normal breathing, I would like you to imagine in the eye of your mind that you are sitting by a beautiful, calm lake. Notice what is around you: the air, the sounds, the colours.

Now notice the birds as they land on the shallow parts of the lake, drinking water, feeding and taking off again. The birds, the lake and the forest are all very calm and peaceful and notice a feeling in your whole body. Breathe in the air.

Notice the thoughts that might be coming to your mind. They can be about anything. Just notice what the thought is about; it could be about dinner, or your shopping list, your children, a family member. Whatever it is, just watch it come out of your mind like a little cloud and place on a bird. Then put the next thought on the next bird and watch them taking off to the sky with the small clouds of your thoughts. Just watch them.

Allow yourself to enjoy this calmness and freedom.

You don't have to engage with the thoughts, just because they are there. Keep breathing the cool, fresh air, enjoy being able to take your thoughts out of your mind and watch them fly away on the birds into the blue sky.

Take a moment to notice the calmness of your body and your mind.

Now start noticing the sounds around you as you are slowly coming back to the room. Whenever you are ready, open your eyes.

How was that for you? How did you feel about being able to take out your thoughts out of your mind and watch them like clouds?

Top tips about self-compassion and mindfulness

- Cultivate self-awareness. Develop a deep understanding of your thoughts, emotions, and reactions.
- Practice self-kindness: Treat yourself with kindness, love, and understanding, just as you would treat a close friend.
- Engage in mindfulness practices such as meditation, deep breathing exercises, or body scans to cultivate present-moment awareness. Pay attention to your

thoughts and emotions without judgment or attachment.

- Challenge the inner critic. Identify and challenge self-critical thoughts by questioning their validity and replacing them with more compassionate and realistic perspectives.
- Get a notebook and practice gratitude. Cultivate a mindset of gratitude by focusing on the positive aspects of your life. Appreciate the small joys, accomplishments, and blessings, which can foster a sense of contentment and self-compassion.

You can download free ebooks, worksheets, audio-guided meditation and attention training at https://www.mindandmood.co.uk/resources/

Chapter 10

Happiness Uncovered:
Beyond the Search

Happiness is a state of mind that can have profound benefits for both physical and mental health. Numerous studies, i.e.. Harvard T.H. Chan School of Public Health, have shown that being in a positive frame of mind can reduce stress, boost the immune system, and increase life expectancy. Additionally, those who experience happiness often report increased feelings of well-being, increased resilience, and even higher levels of productivity.

Unfortunately, we often believe that our happiness is dependent on external factors. We employ socially constructed rules about what will make us happy, and often, happiness is in the future dependent on some conditions. Humans were able to live outdoors, hunting for food for thousands of years. Were they all unhappy?

If only things were different, then we would be happier?

- If only I had a larger house, then I would be happy.
- If I could just get a Porsche, I would be happy.
- If I get this job, I will be over the moon.
- If I got married (had a partner), I would be very happy.
- If I made more money, I would be really happy.
- If I could send my children to a private school, I would be very happy.
- If I could afford these shoes, I would be so happy.

But what happens when they do change? We only feel happy for a bit, then we go back to our baseline. That can be blamed on *Hedonic Adaptation*; we get used to both positive and negative experiences. We may feel really good for a day, a week, a month, or so, but eventually, everything starts feeling normal again. It becomes the new normal.

The truth is that there are no external circumstances that can make us feel good all the time.

It's no wonder that when we're not able to achieve these things, and we compare ourselves to others, we feel disappointed. Especially these days with social media, people post mostly their happiest moments, having dinners, wonderful holidays, and laughing with friends, and we feel everyone else but us are happy. Social media is an illusion; the dinner might have arrived cold, or the return flight might have been delayed, but we rarely see those moments posted.

Happiness is not dependent on any one thing - it's a choice.

What makes us happy?

Research by Kahneman and Deaton (2010) shows that happiness levels bump up as people get a pay increase, however it levels up after $75.000. So emotional well-being rises with income up to but stops at $75.000. That's at the point where you possibly got everything, all basic needs covered in the U.S. They can afford a mortgage, family holidays, decent food, etc. Any income higher than this limit does not seem to make much difference in the level of happiness.

Although people predict that they would be happier if they made $100K or $200K, it seems that the level of happiness comes down to the level of 75K short after, and they are not happy forever as we predict. This is also called Hedonic Adaptation. Everything, good or bad, becomes normalised.

We have more materialistic possessions than what people had in the 1940s (dishwashers, computers, washing machines, mobile phones, even indoor toilets) and yet research shows a slight decrease in happiness levels (Lyubomirsky, 2007) - Is there a correlation between income and happiness? Research shows otherwise.

Average happiness 1940: 7.5 out of 10.
Average happiness 2015: 7.2 out of 10.

Income has gone up, but so did the basic needs. Can this also have anything to do with social media, TV commercials, etc.? Research by Lucas et al. 2003: 25,000 surveys over 15 years show that married couples are happier for the first 1 or 2 years, then they go back to baseline, same as non-married people. We just get used to having what we have.

Most research indicates that thinking and wanting, hoping that the satisfaction will be depending on materialism, apparently has detrimental negative effects on our mental well-being. In their 2003 longitudinal 20 years study, Nickerson, Schwarz, Diener and Kahneman found that people with stronger goals for financial success had less life satisfaction, than those who did not have strong materialistic focus after 20 years.

People, who predicted they would be happier after losing weight and joined a weight loss programme, reported depression after 4 years, compare to those who did not lose weight or gained weight (Jackson et al. 2004, following 2000 obese individuals over 4 years).

The vast amount of research indicates that societal changes over the years, such as increased materialism, social comparison, and individualism, may have contributed to a decline in overall happiness. However, it is important to note that happiness is a complex and multifaceted construct influenced by various individual and societal factors, and not everyone's experience may align with these findings.

We have our everyday life as a baseline. It's different for everyone. But usually you get up, maybe send children to school first and then go to work, then the dinner and kids to bed, sometimes we meet up with family and friends and exercise and so on. That's our everyday life. Then something happens, something amazing, completely out of the ordinary.

For example, landing on a dream job, getting married, arrival of a new baby or we win the lottery! We feel absolutely amazed and happy! But then after a while, even winning the lottery money becomes the new normal and we get used to it. We go back to baseline. We simply do not stay up there of a constant happy state. Emotions come and go as we experience different events.

The good news is, research shows that the same goes for the distressing life events with losses and tragedies, we feel down, sad, and angry, and that's okay. They are all emotions and all part of being human, and just like seasons, emotions keep changing as well. They don't stay the same all the time.

Our emotions play a crucial role in our lives by providing valuable information and guiding our actions. They serve as signals, giving us insight into our inner experiences and reactions to external events. Emotions help us navigate the world by alerting us to potential dangers, highlighting our desires and needs, and connecting us to others.

Sadness allows us to process and heal from loss, disappointment, or grief. It prompts us to reflect on our experiences, learn from them, and seek support from others. Anger alerts us to perceived injustices, violations of boundaries, or situations where our needs are not being met. It can motivate us to take action, assert ourselves, and set healthy boundaries. It is not about getting angry, but what we do with it that matters.

All our emotions contribute to our growth and provide vital insights into our values, needs, and desires. By embracing and honouring these emotions, we can navigate life with greater self-awareness, find meaning, and cultivate a sense of balance and contentment.

Hedonic adaptation

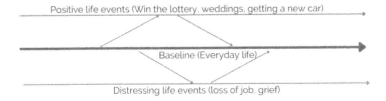

The people that we think are always happy also face tragedy and losses; of course, none of us is immune to negative events and we all do go through difficult times in our lives. Everyone gets their share of hard times. However, some people seem to trust their abilities and strengths to cope with stress and tragedy.

I have listened to a podcast with Mo Gawdat, and he talked about the happiness equation that him and his son had created, and it is quite simply about our expectations from ourselves, others and from the world.

The happiness equation

Expectations met = Happy
Expectations unmet = Unhappy
Expectations over met = Grateful

Looking at this equation, our happiness is directly linked to our expectations. Take a minute to check your expectations to be happy, separate the ones that are within your control and those outside your control. We often expect other people to take certain actions or do things the way we think they should in order to feel happy, but because we cannot control how other people think or behave, we can end up feeling disappointed, upset or even sad.

Happiness is inside of you, and if you start letting go of it being dependent on what other people do or say, you will find it liberating. Only by shifting your expectations, your outlook to life and self-acceptance, you will be able to lead a truly happy and joyful life. And this will positively impact your overall quality of life as well.

Discovering your own happiness can be a challenging and rewarding journey. One way to start is by becoming aware of the small everyday joys available to you. Taking notice of moments that make you smile, like getting a hug from a friend or your child, enjoying your favourite snack, or petting an animal mindfully, watching the sunset, looking at the endless sky or the stars.

Consider yourself lucky for being able to do so, because about 160.000 people did not wake up this morning to experience it. You opened your eyes this morning and were handed a gift of another day.

These simple actions above have the power to bring real happiness into our lives. Not only that, but appreciating these moments helps us forget about our worries for a little bit and gives us some much-needed relief.

Benefits of happiness

The physical benefits associated with happiness are numerous. Studies suggest that those who experience joy and contentment have lower levels of stress hormones, such as cortisol, in their bodies. This can lead to reduced risk for physical illnesses such as heart disease and diabetes. Additionally, individuals who maintain a positive outlook tend to have a stronger immune system, making them less likely to become ill.

The mental benefits associated with feeling happy are also noteworthy. People who regularly experience positive emotions display an improved ability to focus and take on tasks more effectively. Furthermore, those who feel joy and contentment often display increased levels of creativity, allowing them to come up with innovative solutions to problems.

Happiness can have a significant impact on relationships. Studies indicate that people who experience joy and contentment often display greater levels of empathy towards others, leading to improved communication and more meaningful connections with those around them.

Most importantly, remember to always be kind to yourself, as this is a crucial part of increasing happiness in your life. Looking after yourself both mentally and physically will lay the groundwork for greater overall well-being.

Creating habits for happiness

Creating habits that promote and maintain happiness can be an effective way to achieve and sustain a state of contentment. Research has shown that our brains are hard-wired to form patterns and habits, so it's important to establish positive routines that you can stick with over time. Exercise, healthy eating, and socialising are just some of the activities that can help boost your levels of joy.

Exercise: Regular physical activity has been shown to improve physical health, mental clarity, and overall happiness. It can also reduce stress levels, increase energy levels, and improve self-esteem.

Eat Healthy: Eating nutritious foods can help to boost your mood, focus, and energy levels. Incorporating fresh fruits and vegetables into your diet is a great way to get the essential vitamins and minerals needed to function optimally.

Nurture Positive Relationships: Having a strong network of supportive relationships is an important part of feeling happy and fulfilled in life. Spend time with people who lift you up, and who share your values and goals. Make sure to show appreciation for the people you care about, by letting them know how much they mean to you. And if needed, don't be afraid to let go of toxic relationships that no longer serve you.

Cultivate Gratitude: When we express gratitude, it can have a powerful effect on our emotional well-being. Cultivating an attitude of gratitude helps us to recognise and appreciate the blessings in our lives, which can help us feel more positive and hopeful about our future. Make time each day to reflect on what you're thankful for and express your gratitude. You can use a journal, write letters of thanks to people who have made an impact in your life, or even just take a few moments each day to reflect on what you are grateful for. When we choose to focus on the good things in our lives, it can help us to stay positive and motivated to reach our goals.

The recovery rates of people with psychological problems show that those who are taking notes, exploring themselves, working on their journals, goals and gratitude lists have higher rate and quicker recovery, because writing helps you think about it, getting it out and looking for evidence. When things are in our head, they get jumbled up. But putting them on paper, helps you look back at them and have a rethink about them.

Things look different in black and white on paper. So do get yourself a journal, just write down your daily gratitude, your daily positives, your daily intentions until they become a habit. Do this at least for two months, maybe do it once or twice a week. But the research shows that they support more rapid and lasting change.

My Practical Daily Journal "TRANSFORMATION THROUGH THE POWER OF QUOTES: *Daily Mindset Quotes, 5 Minute Planning and Gratitude Journals to Transform Challenges into Triumphs"* is designed exactly for this purpose.

Practice Self-Care. Make sure to prioritise activities that help you relax and recharge. Whether it's taking a hot bath, going for a walk in nature, or indulging in your favourite hobby, make sure to give yourself some time and space each day to do something that brings you joy. Self-care is an important part of staying emotionally healthy, so don't neglect it!

In addition to the above, it's important to practice self-care both mentally and physically. This could include going for regular walks, taking time out for yourself, or even just watching your favourite TV show. Establishing healthy habits like these can help to cultivate a more positive outlook and increase overall happiness levels.

Finally, it is important to remember that increasing happiness is an ongoing process, and you should give yourself time. It's okay to have bad days but try not to get discouraged and keep striving for a more contented life. Trust me, none of us spring out of bed every single day full of happiness.

Thinking and behaviour patterns of happy people according to many researchers (Sonja Lyubomirski, 2007).

- They spend a great amount of quality time with family and friends.
- Express gratitude for everything they have.

- Often first to offer a helping hand to others (but not to the extent of their own wellbeing).
- Practice optimism about their future.
- Weekly or sometimes daily physical exercise routine.
- Committed to lifelong goals and ambitions (i.e. helping animals, fighting fraud, helping people in need, teaching their children deeply held family values).
- They also get stress, tragedy, crisis, but secret weapon is their trust in their abilities and strengths to cope.
- Appreciate pleasures and enjoy the present moment.

Finding meaning and joy in life

Finding lasting happiness involves connecting with something that gives your life purpose and meaning. It's important to assess what it is that truly makes you happy, and then use that as a guide for setting goals and shaping your life around these values. This could be anything from spending time with family, pursuing an education or career path, volunteering in your community, or simply taking up a hobby or pastime.

When it comes to finding joy in life, it's helpful to stay open-minded and try new things. Exploring different cultures, attending local events, or simply taking time out for yourself can help you feel more connected with the world around you and foster a greater sense of well-being.

No matter how small or large, when we actively seek out joy and meaning in our lives it can lead to improved physical health as well as greater mental clarity and focus.

Cultivating resilience and positivity

Having the ability to remain positive in challenging circumstances is an essential part of achieving sustainable happiness. This can be achieved through cultivating resilience or the capacity to cope with difficult situations and recover quickly.

Developing a strong sense of self-awareness is important in order to effectively handle life's ups and downs. Reflecting on both your successes and mistakes can help you build upon your strengths, address any obstacles or weaknesses, and shape a positive mindset for the future.

Finally, being mindful of the present moment can help bring a sense of calmness in times of stress. Practicing meditation or simply taking time out for yourself to relax and reflect is as crucial as physical exercise when it comes to maintaining overall well-being.

Ultimately, happiness is a journey. It doesn't happen overnight - but with patience and commitment, you can create a life that is filled with joy and purpose. By taking small steps each day to cultivate more positivity and gratitude in your life, you will be well on your way to achieving a greater sense of happiness and contentment.

Building and sustaining happiness

Now that you have explored various techniques for increasing happiness levels, it is important to make a conscious effort to maintain this mindset. Staying connected with the things that bring joy to your life can help you form and sustain positive habits.

When it comes to building upon happiness, try using goal setting as a tool for personal growth. Writing down achievable goals and tasks based on what gives you purpose and meaning will help keep motivation levels high.

Practice self-care, such as taking time out for yourself to relax and refuel. This could be anything from a quiet moment of reflection to any number of activities that bring joy, such as reading a book, going for a walk or spending time with friends.

Finally, remember that feelings of happiness come in waves, so stay mindful of your emotions. Even when life gets difficult, start training your mind to find the silver lining and remember that there is still joy to be found.

If you have ever experienced happiness, it is inside you, so perhaps it is time to look inside rather than searching for it outside. When you can choose to be happy right now rather than looking for perfection in everything or delaying for something in the future, then you will find yourself in a position where anything else becomes an added bonus on top of that choice.

"Thank you".

It has been an honour to be a part of your journey. I hope you enjoyed reading my book as much as I enjoyed writing it. If you found it helpful, please do share your thoughts on Amazon, so we can spread the word for others who can benefit.

Aylin's programme feedback from clients:

Aylin's coaching sessions have made a huge positive impact in my life. EMDR really helped to process the loss of my parents and my fear of water. I am now able to enjoy swimming with my children. My expectations are much more realistic from myself and others, and when something goes wrong, I am much calmer. I also have much more confidence in myself and able to set boundaries. It has been great & helpful, thank you". - Rachel C

"I used to be very harsh on myself before I started my coaching sessions with Aylin. I have now become more aware of my inner critical voice, and I am a lot more tolerant with myself. I don't put my self-worth on my high demands of myself any longer. I know I am worthwhile, so I also take time to look after myself, and can let go when everything is not what I used to perceive as "perfect". Thank you Aylin" - Daniela.

Aylin is by far the best therapist I've seen. She was truly helpful and insightful and challenged me and helped me change some of the thought patterns I've had my whole life. She didn't just listen she gave very constructive advice and helped me support myself better. Thank you so much for everything! - Client Google review:

Aylin is wonderful at helping you take control of your thoughts and feelings and channel it all into something positive. Aylin is so kind and comfortable to be around. My sessions with Aylin have helped change my life for the better. I highly recommend. Cheryl G -

Client William Locker: Aylin is a brilliant coach, she guided me toward a new way of thinking. And in fact, I actually talk to people about our zoom sessions all the time as I apply the things I am learning to my everyday life. CBT has changed my life for the better and I can honestly say that I am the happiest and most confident in myself that I have ever been. For anyone struggling with these issues, I couldn't recommend Aylin Webb CBT more highly. Thank you Aylin!

Book reviews:
Transformation Through the Power Of Quotes: *Daily Mindset Quotes, 5 Minute Planning and Gratitude Journals to Transform Challenges into Triumphs*

Joanna C-D
I love it!
Inspirational book of quotations by famous people, brilliantly designed in a 10-week program by Aylin. Uplifting, motivational and very easy to apply in our busy schedules. I keep it in my bag for everyday journeys on tubes or buses. It gives me a moment of calm reflection and tranquillity. Thank you, Aylin. Highly recommended.

BJose
A must have for anyone who loves quotes.
Love this! A nice amount of thought-provoking workbook material to compliment the quotes. I definitely recommend this to anyone who loves quotes and who might be looking to work through some thoughts.

Vickie N
Brilliant!
I love it! Not just jam packed with brilliant thought-provoking quotes, but it has really useful practical application. Its proving useful already. I'll be recommending this to my own clients for sure

Ozlem Sen
Such a great idea!
This book is an amazing helper to turn yourself into an achiever. Such a great idea to pull all these wonderful quotes together in a book and even a better idea to use them with a plan to transform yourself! I enjoyed every word of the book. Every page put a smile on my face and me start my day with motivation and dedication. Thanks so much Aylin Webb!

EDJ
A fantastic guide with inspirational quotes.
This book is so clear and easy to use. The workbook style structure helps to handrail a journey guided by words from some of the world's most inspirational people. I would highly recommend this book to anyone.

You can find out more about Aylin and her works on her website www.mindandmood.co.uk and listen to her podcast "I am a perfectionist, get me out of here" https://aylinwebb.buzzsprout.com, _which_ had over 22000 downloads within a year.

Podcast reviews:

Very insightful and helpful
J.C. Jones
Aylin is brilliant! This is an excellent podcast, it has been very illuminating and insightful in helping me to understand what perfectionism is, the implications behind it, and how to accept and overcome it. Highly recommended!

I really enjoyed the show!
Robertsilvers33
Thank you for all the insights, I love to learn from you!

Awesome show!
josephdoan22
Love your show. So many great tips!

For further info and testimonials, go to www.mindandmood.co.uk.

You can download free ebooks, worksheets, audio-guided meditation and attention training at https://www.mindandmood.co.uk/resources/

About the Author

Aylin, an experienced psychologist (MSc) and 5-star book author, has been a guiding light for individuals battling anxiety, helping them foster confidence through her acclaimed 7-step Signature Programme developed over the past decade. With a rich history that spans from Istanbul to Denmark and finally settling in London, she has utilised her background in TV production, spanning 15 years, to build a formidable career as an Accredited Coach, CBT and EMDR Therapist, NLP Practitioner and Podcaster. Aylin is also the author of a previously published practical manual. She invites people to transformative experiences through her highly praised book "Transformation Through The Power of Quotes" and her rapidly growing podcast, "I am A Perfectionist, Get Me Out Of Here," which has already captivated over 24,000 listeners and continues to expand its audience. Embark on a journey of self-discovery with Aylin and unlock a life filled with confidence, joy, and vibrant energy. Visit http://www.mindandmood.co.uk to explore her enriching world.

Printed in Great Britain
by Amazon

29138663R00116